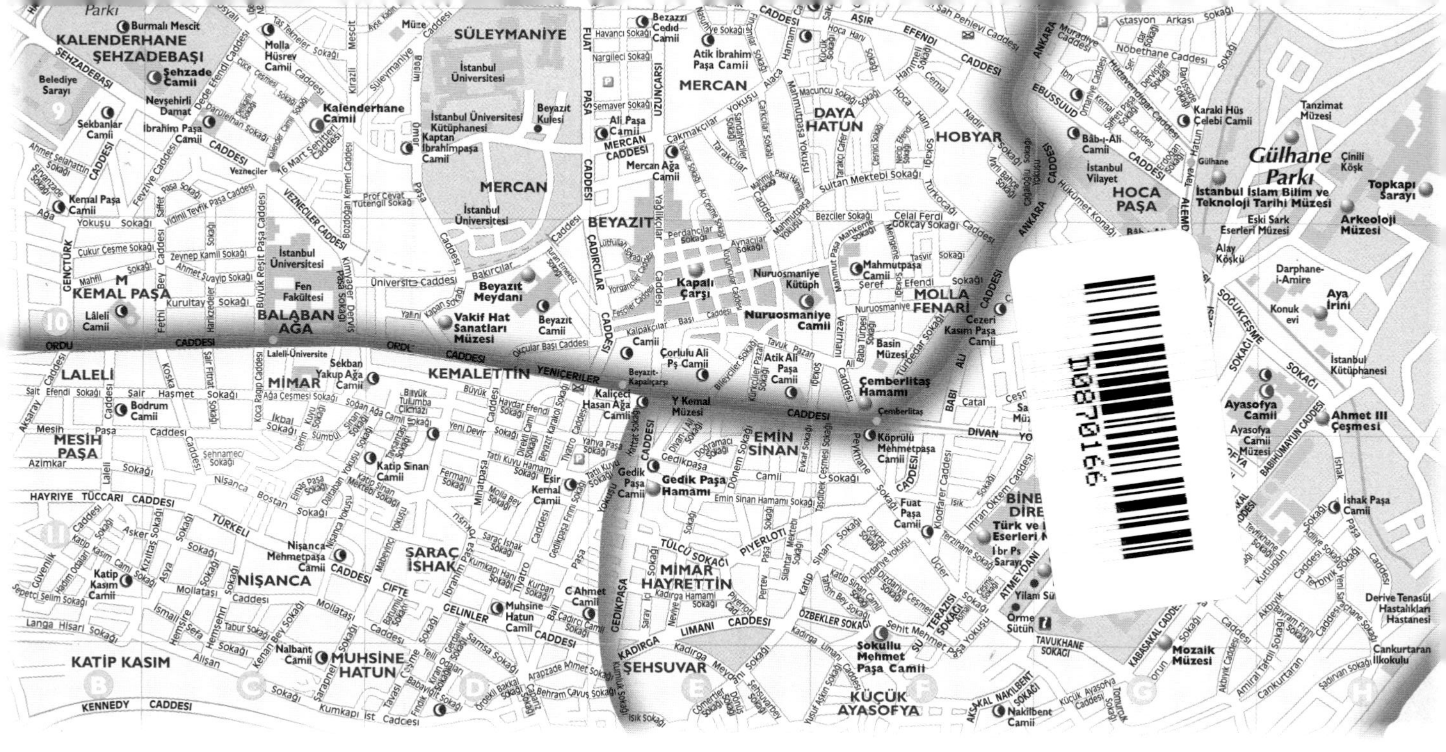
KALENDERHANE
ŞEHZADEBAŞI
SÜLEYMANİYE
MERCAN
DAYA HATUN
HOBYAR
HOCA PAŞA
Gülhane Parkı
Topkapı Sarayı
Arkeoloji Müzesi
İstanbul İslam Bilim ve Teknoloji Tarihi Müzesi
BEYAZIT
Kapalı Çarşı
Nuruosmaniye Camii
MOLLA FENARİ
Aya İrini
Ayasofya Camii
Ahmet III Çeşmesi
Beyazıt Meydanı
Vakıf Hat Sanatları Müzesi
BALABAN AĞA
M KEMAL PAŞA
LALELİ
MİMAR
KEMALETTİN
Çemberlitaş Hamamı
EMİN SİNAN
Gedik Paşa Hamamı
MESİH PAŞA
SARAÇ İSHAK
NİŞANCA
MİMAR HAYRETTİN
ŞEHSUVAR
Sokullu Mehmet Paşa Camii
KÜÇÜK AYASOFYA
Mozaik Müzesi
MUHSİNE HATUN
KATİP KASIM
ORDU CADDESİ
KENNEDY CADDESİ
ANKARA CADDESİ
DIVAN YOLU
D0870166

Fodor's

25 Best

ISTANBUL

How to Use This Book

KEY TO SYMBOLS

- Map reference to the accompanying fold-out map
- Address
- Telephone number
- Opening/closing times
- Restaurant or café
- Nearest rail station
- Nearest subway (Metro) station
- Nearest bus route
- Nearest riverboat or ferry stop
- Facilities for visitors with disabilities
- Other practical information
- Further information
- Tourist information
- Admission charges: Expensive (over $6), Moderate ($3–$6) and Inexpensive ($3 or less)

This guide is divided into four sections

• Essential Istanbul: An introduction to the city and tips on making the most of your stay.

• Istanbul by Area: We've broken the city into five areas, and recommended the best sights, shops, entertainment venues, nightlife and restaurants in each one. Suggested walks help you to explore on foot.

• Where to Stay: The best hotels, whether you're looking for luxury, budget or something in between.

• Need to Know: The info you need to make your trip run smoothly, including getting about by public transport, weather tips, emergency phone numbers and useful websites.

Navigation In the Istanbul by Area chapter, we've given each area its own color, which is also used on the locator maps throughout the book and the map on the inside front cover.

Maps The fold-out map with this book is a comprehensive street plan of Istanbul. The grid on this fold-out map is the same as the grid on the locator maps within the book. We've given grid references within the book for each sight and listing.

Contents

Introducing Istanbul

Istanbul, Byzantium, Constantinople—whatever you call it, this city has always excited the imagination. Once home to two of the world's greatest empires, it straddles the Bosphorus like a bridge between continents, with Europe on one side and Asia on the other.

At first glance, Istanbul is full of contradictions. It's a city of mosques and minarets but it's also the spiritual home of the Orthodox church. It's not even the capital of Turkey—a largely Asian, Muslim country—but could soon be the biggest metropolis in the European Union. Old women in headscarves wander the streets of Fener, while young women in miniskirts stroll along Istiklâl Caddesi and drink in trendy bars on their way to the latest opening at Istanbul Modern. It may be a cliché, but Istanbul seems torn between ancient and modern, east and west.

Look more closely and you see a confident, forward-looking city, which is rediscovering its Ottoman heritage at the same time as embracing Europe. In music, art, fashion and cuisine, young Turks are seeking inspiration from the past to create a 21st-century Ottoman chic. Most visitors are attracted by the beauty of the Blue Mosque, but the legacy of the Ottoman empire is more than just a collection of monuments.

At the junction of the Golden Horn and the Bosphorus, Istanbul is a city on the water. Stand on the dockside at Eminönü, beneath the Galata Bridge, at dusk. The scent of grilled mackerel mingles with the soundtrack of city life, as taxi horns, honking ferries and Arabesque music almost drown out the call to prayer from a thousand minarets. As the sun sets over the water and the domes of Istanbul are silhouetted against the sky, it is impossible not to be seduced by this unique city.

Facts + Figures

- Population: 13,900,000 (2013)
- Growth rate: 1.68 percent per year
- Annual visitors: 9.5 million (2012)
- Mobile phone use: 90 percent
- Mosques: 3,000

BRIDGING THE GAP

The 1.5km (1 mile) Bosphorus suspension bridge, opened in 1973 between Beylerbeyi and Ortaköy, carries more than 180,000 vehicles between Europe and Asia each day. At one time, pedestrians were allowed to walk across, but this is no longer permitted due to the high number of suicide attempts.

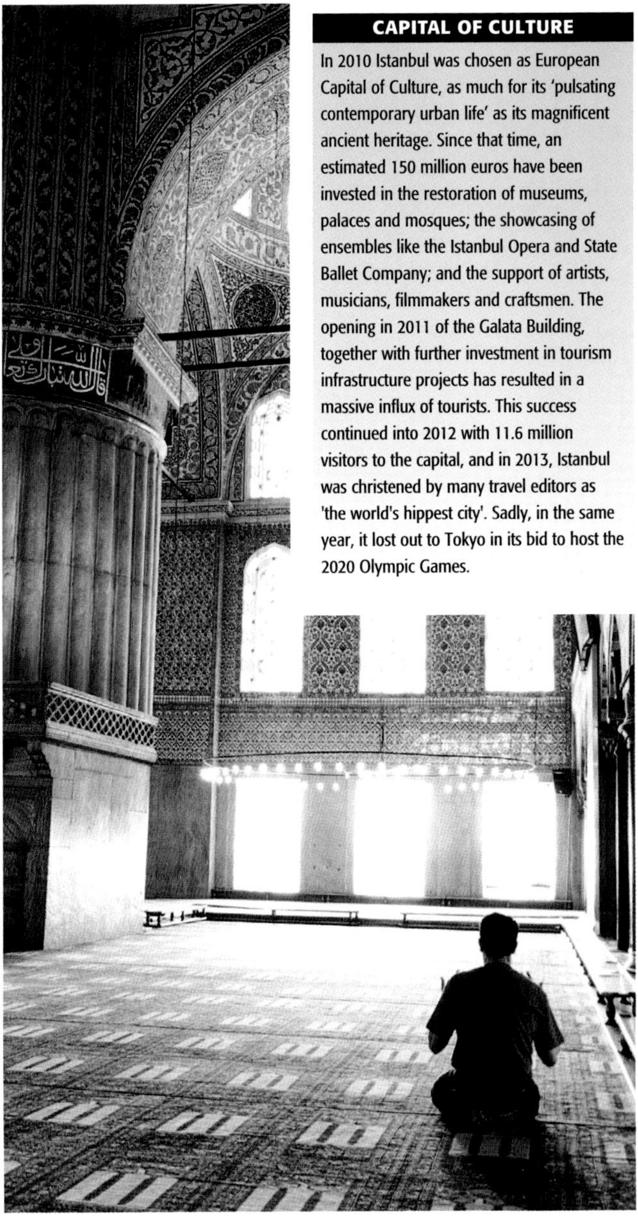

CAPITAL OF CULTURE

In 2010 Istanbul was chosen as European Capital of Culture, as much for its 'pulsating contemporary urban life' as its magnificent ancient heritage. Since that time, an estimated 150 million euros have been invested in the restoration of museums, palaces and mosques; the showcasing of ensembles like the Istanbul Opera and State Ballet Company; and the support of artists, musicians, filmmakers and craftsmen. The opening in 2011 of the Galata Building, together with further investment in tourism infrastructure projects has resulted in a massive influx of tourists. This success continued into 2012 with 11.6 million visitors to the capital, and in 2013, Istanbul was christened by many travel editors as 'the world's hippest city'. Sadly, in the same year, it lost out to Tokyo in its bid to host the 2020 Olympic Games.

A Short Stay in Istanbul

DAY 1

Morning Explore the main sights of Sultanahmet. The best place to get your bearings is **At Meydanı** (the Hippodrome, ▷ 25), which is well placed for visiting the **Sultanahmet Camii** (Blue Mosque, ▷ 32).

Mid-morning Enjoy a Turkish tea or coffee at **Derviş Aile Cay Bahçesi** (▷ 43), opposite the Blue Mosque, then cross the park to **Ayasofya Camii** (▷ 26–27) to admire the mosaics of this magnificent Byzantine church. Afterwards, you can visit **Yerebatan Sarnıcı** (▷ 37), a vast, atmospheric underground cathedral of water.

Lunch There are several lunchtime options near the foot of **Divan Yolu** (▷ 38), but for an inexpensive, classic Turkish snack, try the köfte (meat-balls) at **Tarihi Sultanahmet Köftecisi** (▷ 44).

Afternoon Walk or take the tram up Divan Yolu to Beyazıt, then spend a couple of hours shopping in the **Kapalı Çarşı** (Grand Bazaar, ▷ 50–51), which has some 3,000 stores and enjoys around 3,500 visitors a day. Afterwards treat yourself to a steam bath and massage at **Çemberlitaş Hamamı** (▷ 49), a beautiful Turkish bath designed by Mimar Sinan.

Early evening Take the tram to Eminönü and hop on a ferry to **Üsküdar** (▷ 101), then stroll along the waterfront to **Kız Kulesi** (▷ 100) to admire the views.

Dinner Stay in Üsküdar for dinner at **Kanaat** (▷ 106), a historic *lokanta* and Istanbul institution. Alternatively, take the ferry back to Eminönü and cross the road to **Hamdi Et Lokantası** (▷ 62).

Evening Relax with a drink at a café beneath **Galata Bridge** (▷ 56).

DAY 2

Morning Arrive at the **Topkapı Sarayı** (Topkapı Palace, ▷ 34–35) at 9am, when the gates open, and allow a whole morning for your visit. It's impossible to see everything in one visit, so concentrate on the Treasury, imperial costumes, collection of arms and the relics of the Prophet Muhammad. Take the guided tour of the Harem for a fascinating insight into the lives of the sultans and the Ottoman court.

Lunch Konyalı (▷ 44), in the palace gardens, is a popular spot for lunch, so get there early for a table on the terrace, with views over the Bosphorus.

Afternoon Stroll through the grounds of Topkapı Palace to **Gülhane Parkı** (▷ 39), with its views of the Bosphorus, then take the tram across Galata Bridge to **Tophane Meydanı** (▷ 84). For a complete contrast to Topkapı, visit **Istanbul Modern** (▷ 78–79).

Early evening Continue on the tram to Kabataş, then transfer to the funicular for the short ascent to **Taksim Meydanı** (▷ 84). From here, you can join the early-evening promenade along **Istiklâl Caddesi** (▷ 80–81).

Dinner Enjoy a feast of mezes washed down with rakı at one of the *meyhanes* along **Nevizade Soka i** (▷ 88–89) or **Çiçek Pasajı** (▷ 82).

Evening Stay in Beyoğlu to catch some live music at the bars and clubs off Istiklâl Caddesi. Depending on your taste in music, you could hear jazz at **Nardis** (▷ 87), rock at **Babylon** (▷ 86), Anatolian *saz* at **Munzur** (▷ 87), or take in a classical performance at **Akbank Sanat** (▷ 86).

Top 25

Arkeoloji Müzesi ▷ 24 The Archaeological Museum is packed with treasures of the ancient Orient.

At Meydanı ▷ 25 This elongated square stands on the site of the ancient Roman Hippodrome.

Ayasofya Camii ▷ 26–27 Istanbul's famous basilica is decorated with lovely mosaics.

Beyazıt Meydanı ▷ 48 Istanbul's busiest square is graced by a beautiful 16th-century mosque.

Beylerbeyi Sarayı ▷ 94 This was the sultans' summer palace from 1861. It's small but sumptuous.

Boğaziçi ▷ 95 Take a Bosphorus cruise to escape the dust and crowds, and see waterfront mansions.

Çemberlitaş Hamamı ▷ 49 Magnificent 16th-century Ottoman baths designed by Mimar Sinan.

Dolmabahçe Sarayı ▷ 96–97 No expense was spared in the construction of this vast, gaudy palace.

Eyüp Sultan Camii ▷ 66–67 Popular mosque, decorated in Ottoman baroque style.

Istanbul Modern ▷ 78–79 Turkey's first private museum of modern art, founded in 2004.

Istiklâl Caddesi ▷ 80–81 The city's main shopping street is also known for its nightlife.

Kapalı Çarşı ▷ 50–51 The Grand Bazaar is a bustling labyrinth with more than 3,500 shops.

Kariye Camii ▷ 68–69 Byzantine mosaics and frescoes in a late 14th-century church.

Küçük Ayasofya Camii ▷ 28 Istanbul's oldest mosque is distinguished by its intriguing design.

Mısır Çarşısı ▷ 52 Come to the Spice Bazaar for spices, sweets—and aphrodisiacs.

Mozaik Müzesi ▷ 29 Mosaics recovered from Constantine's imperial palace are displayed here.

Rüstem Paşa Camii ▷ 53 Beautifully tiled mosque designed by master architect Mimar Sinan.

Sokullu Mehmet Paşa Camii ▷ 30–31 Stunning Sinan mosque with lovely tiled mihrab wall.

Süleymaniye Camii ▷ 54–55 Süleyman the Magnificent is buried in Sinan's finest mosque.

Sultanahmet Camii ▷ 32–33 The Blue Mosque dominates the skyline of old Istanbul; inside are the 20,000 azure tiles that give it its nickname.

Topkapı Sarayı ▷ 34–35 The headquarters of the Ottoman Empire for 400 years is now an important museum.

Türk ve Islam Eserleri Müzesi ▷ 36 Varied collection of Eastern arts from ceramics to textiles.

Yedikule Hisarı ▷ 70 Explore the old Byzantine fortifications and enjoy the splendid views over the city.

Yerebatan Sarnıcı ▷ 37 Vast underground chamber, known as the Sunken Palace, built by Emperor Justinian to store water.

Yıldız Parkı ▷ 98 Wooded parkland around Yıldız Palace that's a popular retreat from the city.

These pages are a quick guide to the Top 25, which are described in more detail later. Here they are listed alphabetically. The tinted background shows the area they are in.

Shopping

Istanbul provides retail therapy for even the most jaded shopper. Few people leave without a souvenir, whether it's a hand-woven Turkish carpet or a box of *lokum* (Turkish delight).

Souvenirs range from traditional Turkish dolls and water pipes to brightly embroidered slippers

The Bazaars

The ultimate shopping experience is the Grand Bazaar (⊳ 50–51), in business since the Ottoman conquest. Entire streets are dedicated to jewelry, leather and clothes. Among the items on sale are carpets, *kilims* (flat-woven rugs), ceramic tiles, gold and silver, meerschaum pipes, silk and cotton clothing, backgammon and chess sets, jewelry boxes, belly-dancing costumes and *nargiles* (water pipes, ⊳ panel, 86).

Shopping in the bazaar is great fun but it has become something of a game, with pushy traders enticing you into their shops and potential customers attempting to resist their charms. Most of what is on sale in the bazaar these days is aimed at tourists, and most locals prefer to shop in the Tahtakale district, between the Grand and Spice bazaars. The streets here are always crowded with shoppers searching for inexpensive clothes.

Meanwhile, if you want to buy a carpet but find the Grand Bazaar a bit intimidating, the Arasta Bazaar, beside the Blue Mosque, has a row of smart shops in a former stable turned shopping arcade, offering a fantastic range of high-quality carpets, rugs, jewelry

THE EVIL EYE

A popular souvenir is a *nazar bonjuk*, a good-luck charm, which is supposed to protect the wearer against the 'evil eye'. Made out of blown glass with a blue 'eye' in the center, you'll find these being sold all over Istanbul as bracelets, earrings and pins. The tradition of wearing of them is based on a superstition that one person can cast a spell on another simply by looking at them. No one really believes this any more, but many people still wear a *nazar bonjuk* just in case.

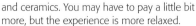

and ceramics. You may have to pay a little bit more, but the experience is more relaxed.

Herbs and spices, dried fruits, scented teas and Turkish delight can all be found in the Spice Bazaar (▷ 52). There are excellent specialist food shops and delicatessens on and around Güneşlibahçe Sokaği, a short walk from the ferry terminal in Kadıköy. Come here for bread, cheese, sausages, yogurt, olives, olive oil and honey. Kadıköy also hosts the biggest street market, which takes place every Tuesday morning if you want to join the crowds.

Shopping Districts

Istanbul has a superb range of specialist shopping areas. For old books and calligraphy, head for the Sahaflar Çarşısı, located in a courtyard behind Beyazıt mosque. The main street of Beyoğlu, Istiklâl Caddesi (▷ 80–81), has a wealth of bookshops, music and clothes stores. Galip Dede Caddesi is the place to go for musical instruments, while the Çukurcuma district is known for its antiques shops. Fashion-lovers should head to the upscale districts of Nişantaşı and Teşvikiye, with their upmarket designer boutiques. The big American-style shopping malls, such as Akmerkez, Kanyon and Metrocity, are farther north, near the Levent Metro station, and offer a range of stores and places to eat.

STRIKING A BARGAIN

Few goods in Istanbul's shops and bazaars are fixed price and the amount you pay will come down to bargaining. Many visitors find this custom irritating but, if you stay polite and good-natured, it is all part of the fun. The shopkeeper will start at a price well above what he is prepared to accept; the customer will offer much less and eventually they will meet in the middle. With major purchases such as a carpet, the process can be drawn out over endless cups of tea. In the end, remember that what matters is not whether you pay the lowest price but that you buy something you like at a price that you are happy with.

Shopping by Theme

Whether you want to hunt for bargains in bazaars or seek out the latest fashions in designer boutiques, you'll find it all in Istanbul. On this page shops are listed by theme. For more detailed information, see the listings in Istanbul by Area.

ANTIQUES

Anadol Antik (▷ 85)
Antikarnas (▷ 85)
Popcorn (▷ 85)
Sofa (▷ 60)

BATH ACCESSORIES

Abdulla (▷ 59)
Derviş (▷ 59)

BAZAARS

Arasta Çarşısı (▷ 42)
Kapalı Çarşı (▷ 50)
Mısır Çarşısı (▷ 52)
Sahaflar Çarşısı (▷ 60)

BOOKS

Galeri Kayseri (▷ 42)
Homer (▷ 85)
Librairie de Péra (▷ 85)
Robinson Crusoe (▷ 85)
Sahaflar Çarşısı (▷ 60)

CARPETS AND KILIMS

Adnan & Hasan (▷ 59)
Elegance (▷ 42)
Ethnicon (▷ 59)
Galeri Cengiz (▷ 42)
Punto (▷ 60)
Şengör (▷ 60)
Şişko Osman (▷ 60)

CERAMICS

CS Iznik Nicea Ceramics (▷ 59)
Iznik Tiles (▷ 42)
Yıldız Porselen Fabrikası (▷ 104)

CRAFTS

Dösim BKG (▷ 42)
Istanbul Handicrafts Centre (▷ 42)
Silk and Cashmere (▷ 60)
La Tienda (▷ 60)

FASHION

Cocoon (▷ 42)
Galeri Cengiz (▷ 42)
Gönül Paksoy (▷ 85)
Koç Deri (▷ 59)
Mavi Jeans (▷ 85)
Steel Leather (▷ 42)

FOOD AND DRINK

Ali Muhiddin Hacı Bekir (▷ 59)
Kurakahveci Mehmet Efendi (▷ 59)
Malatya Pazarı (▷ 59)
Mısır Çarşısı (▷ 52)
Vefa (▷ 60)

GLASS

Paşabahçe (▷ 85)

JEWELRY

Damas (▷ 104)

MUSIC

Istanbul Müzik Merkezi (▷ 85)
Megavizyon (▷ 85)

SHOPPING MALLS

Akmerkez (▷ 104)
Kanyon (▷ 104)

Istanbul by Night

Watch some dancing, browse a night market or enjoy a meal alfresco

If most visitors to Istanbul spend their days in Sultanahmet exploring museums, mosques and bazaars, then Beyoşlu, on the far side of the Galata Bridge, is definitely the place to go after dark.

Plenty of Choice

On summer evenings, Istiklâl Caddesi resembles an endless fashion parade and music pours out of countless bars. From intimate jazz clubs and live folk music venues to rowdy *meyhanes* where fasıl musicians tour the tables while the customers knock back the *rakı*, you are bound to find something that appeals.

Summer by the Sea

In summer, the clubbing crowd moves down to the Bosphorus, to open-air megaclubs in Ortaköy and Kuruçeşme, either side of the Bosphorus Bridge. If you prefer caffeine to alcohol, head for one of the many *çay bahçesis* (tea gardens) to sip coffee.

Night Light

Sultanahmet is mostly quiet after dark, apart from the backpacker bars along Akbıyık Caddesi. However, the Blue Mosque is brilliantly illuminated at night and there are few experiences to beat sitting on a terrace with a view of the Blue Mosque as the call to prayer drifts across the city.

AN EVENING STROLL

Take the ferry from Sirkeci to Harem on the Asian shore. Behind the landing stage are the Selimiye barracks, where the British nurse, Florence Nightingale, famously set up her hospital during the Crimean War and established new standards in patient care. Walk northwards along the waterfront promenade, with views of the Topkapı Palace, Ayasofya and Blue Mosque. On an island at the entrance to the Bosphorus, the 18th-century Kız Kulesi (Maiden's Tower, ▷ 100) comes into view. Continue walking to reach Üsküdar, where you can catch a ferry back to Eminönü.

Eating Out

From barbecued fish on the quayside at Eminönü to romantic restaurants serving new-wave fusion cuisine, Istanbul offers a full range of dining experiences.

What to Eat

Gone are the days when eating out in Turkey meant a *döner kebap* from a street stall, although you will still find these all over the city. Traditional Turkish cooking is based on fresh local ingredients, especially lamb, fish and vegetables, while modern Turkish cuisine blends Turkish and global influences.

Where to Eat

A *restoran* is a formal restaurant, while a *lokanta* is more casual, serving ready-prepared meals and grilled meat, but usually no alcohol. *Meyhanes* (▷ 88) are taverns offering tapas-like *mezes* to share, while *pide salonu* specialize in *pide,* a pizza-type flatbread. For fresh fish, head for Kumkapı (▷ 44) or the villages beside the Bosphorus.

Practicalities

Most restaurants open from around noon to midnight. Since 2009 smoking has been banned from enclosed public places (see notices in restaurants); violations are punished by a fine. Tipping is expected; it is usual to add 10 percent.

TASTY TURKISH DISHES

Arnavut ciğeri—spicy liver with onions
Çerkez tavuğu—chicken in walnut purée
Döner kebap—lamb grilled on a spit
Iç pilav—rice with nuts, currants and onions
Mantı—ravioli with yoghurt
Piyaz—haricot bean salad
Sigara böreği—fried filo pastry filled with cheese
Şiş köfte—grilled meatballs
Su böreği—baked pastry filled with meat or cheese
Tas kebap—vegetable and meat stew
Yaprak dolma—stuffed vine leaves

If you're in a hurry, try a takeout kebab, a snack from a street stand or a pastry or delicious dessert

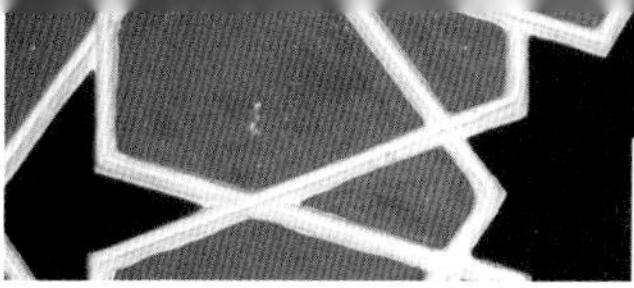

Restaurants by Cuisine

Istanbul has restaurants to suit all tastes and budgets. On this page they are listed by cuisine. For more detailed descriptions, see the individual listings in Istanbul by Area.

ASIAN

Banyan (▷ 105)

FISH AND SEAFOOD

Aquarius (▷ 105)
Asmalımescit Balikçısı (▷ 88)
Baba (▷ 105)
Beyaz (▷ 44)
Botanik (▷ 105)
Çinaraltı (▷ 105)
Deniz Kızı (▷ 105)
Gözde (▷ 106)
Kavak Doğanay (▷ 106)
Rumeli Iskele (▷ 106)
Yelken (▷ 106)
Yoros Café (▷ 106)

FRENCH

Café du Levant (▷ 74)

FUSION/TRENDY

Lokanta (▷ 90)
Mikla (▷ 90)
Müzedechanga (▷ 106)
Vogue (▷ 106)

MEDITERRANEAN

A'Jia (▷ 105)

RUSSIAN

Galata Evi (▷ 88)

SPANISH

Venta del Toro (▷ 90)

SWEETS

Asırlık Kanlıca Yoğurdu (▷ 105)
Mado (▷ 90)

TURKISH: GRILLED MEAT

Aya Yorgi Manastiri (▷ 105)
Develi (▷ 74)
Doy-Doy (▷ 44)
Hamdi Et Lokantası (▷ 62)
Tarihi Sultanahmet Köftecisi (▷ 44)

TURKISH: *LOKANTA*

Hacı Abdullah (▷ 88)
Kanaat (▷ 106)

TURKISH: *MEYHANE*

Boncuk (▷ 88)
Imroz (▷ 88)
Neyle Meyle (▷ 90)
Palmiye (▷ 90)
Refik (▷ 90)
Sofyalı 9 (▷ 90)

TURKISH: REGIONAL

Cennet (▷ 44)
Ficcin (▷ 88)
Otantik (▷ 90)

TURKISH: SNACKS

Kariye Pembe Köşk (▷ 74)

TURKISH: TRADITIONAL

Aloran (▷ 44)
Asitane (▷ 74)
Darüzziyafe (▷ 62)
Konyalı (▷ 44)
Pandeli (▷ 62)
Rami (▷ 44)
Sarniç (▷ 44)
Tarihi Haliç Işkembecişi (▷ 74)

VEGETARIAN

Cooking Alaturka (▷ 88)

Top Tips For...

However you'd like to spend your time in Istanbul, these top suggestions should help you tailor your ideal visit. Each suggestion has a fuller write-up elsewhere in the book.

CATCHING LOCAL MUSIC

Join a lively late-night crowd to hear Anatolian folk musicians at Munzur (▷ 87).
See the whirling dervishes at Galata Mevlevihanesi (▷ 86).
Spend an evening at Kumkapı (▷ panel, 44), being serenaded by *fasıl* musicians.

Inside Sokullu Mehmet Paşa Mosque (above); whirling dervishes (top)

ISLAMIC ART AND ARCHITECTURE

Marvel at the Iznik tiles at the exquisite Rüstem Paşa Mosque (▷ 53).
Visit Sokullu Mehmet Paşa Mosque (▷ 30–31), one of Mimar Sinan's finest creations.
Explore the history of Islamic art at the Museum of Turkish and Islamic Art (▷ 36).
Relax in a historic Turkish bath at Çemberlitaş Hamamı (▷ 49).

WATERSIDE DINING

Enjoy fresh fish beside the Bosphorus in the garden at Yelken (▷ 106).
Take the ferry to Anadolu Kavağı for lunch at Baba (▷ 105).
Take your pick of the many restaurants beneath Galata Bridge (▷ 56).

OTTOMAN CHIC

Taste new versions of classic Ottoman dishes at Asitane (▷ 74).
Stay in a restored Ottoman house, such as Empress Zoe hotel (▷ 110).
Buy shirts and bath towels inspired by Ottoman designs at Derviş (▷ 59).

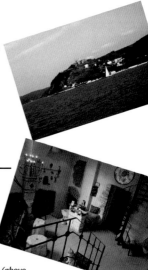

A yacht passes the hilltop castle at Anadolu Kavağı (above right); experience some Ottoman chic at Empress Zoe hotel (right)

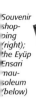

Souvenir shopping (right); the Eyüp Ensari mausoleum (below)

BARGAIN-HUNTING

Browse the antiques shops of Çukurcuma (▷ 82).
Visit Ortaköy (▷ 100) on Sunday morning, when artists sell their work in the street.
Go prepared to haggle for everything from Turkish carpets to chess sets in the Grand Bazaar (▷ 50–51).
Pick up Turkish CDs at bargain prices in the shops on Istiklâl Caddesi (▷ 80–81).

MEETING THE LOCALS

Check out the food shops and delicatessens at Kadıköy (▷ 100).
Make the pilgrimage to Eyüp (▷ 66–67) and join the pilgrims at the mausoleum.
Join the early-evening promenade along Istiklâl Caddesi (▷ 80–81).
Drink tea and play backgammon in a traditional Turkish café like Yeni Marmara (▷ 43).

Across the Bosphorus (above)

GETTING AWAY FROM IT ALL

Leave the city behind by taking the boat to the Princes' Islands in summer (▷ 102).
Take a picnic to Yıldız Park (▷ 98).
Stroll through Gülhane Park (▷ 39) for tea overlooking the Bosphorus at Set Üstü (▷ 43).
Cruise the Bosphorus (▷ 95).

SLEEPING IN STYLE

Live the high life in a wooden mansion at Les Ottomans (▷ 112).
Sleep like a sultan at the Çirağan Palace Kempinski (▷ 112).
Follow in Agatha Christie's footsteps at the Pera Palas (▷ 83).

The Çirağan Palace at Beşiktaş is now a luxury hotel (left)

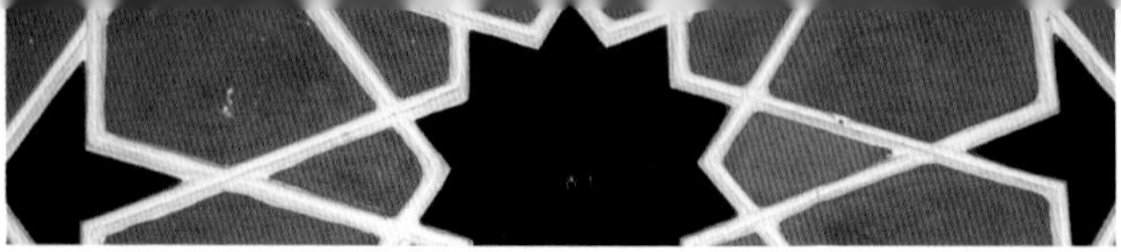

BIRD'S-EYE VIEWS

View from the top of the Galata Tower

Ride the cable car to the Pierre Loti Café (▷ 66), overlooking the Golden Horn.
Visit the observation platform at the top of Galata Tower (▷ 82–83).
Climb to the ruined castle above Anadolu Kavağı (▷ 99) for views of the Bosphorus and Black Sea.
Take a taxi to Büyük Çamlıca (▷ 99) to gaze over the city.

SAMPLING LOCAL FOOD

Feast on delicious mezes and *pide* bread at Develi (▷ 74).
Tuck into the house special at Hacı Abdullah (▷ 88), the best of Istanbul's *lokantas*.
Enjoy grilled mackerel from the night barbecues at Eminönü (▷ panel, 62).

SOMETHING FOR NOTHING

Take advantage of free admission on Thursdays at Istanbul Modern (▷ 78–79).
Visit the Blue Mosque (▷ 32–33)—entry to mosques is free but a donation is appreciated.
Soak up the atmosphere of the carpet auction on Wednesday in the Grand Bazaar (▷ 50–51).
Take the ferry along the Golden Horn (▷ 71)—not quite free but worth it for the views alone.

Locally caught fish (top); the Blue Mosque (above)

KEEPING THE KIDS HAPPY

Walk through a miniature version of Turkey at Miniatürk (▷ 72).
Relive your childhood at Istanbul Toy Museum (▷ 100).
Gorge on free samples of Turkish delight at the Spice Bazaar (▷ 52).

Don't leave Istanbul without trying some Turkish delight (right)

Istanbul by Area

SULTANAHMET

EMINÖNÜ AND BAZAAR QUARTER

WESTERN DISTRICTS

BEYOĞLU

FARTHER AFIELD

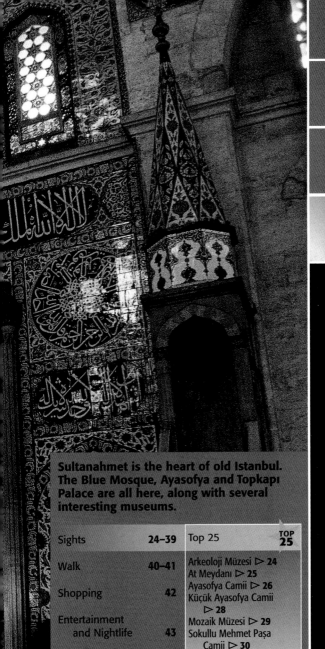

Sultanahmet

Sultanahmet is the heart of old Istanbul. The Blue Mosque, Ayasofya and Topkapı Palace are all here, along with several interesting museums.

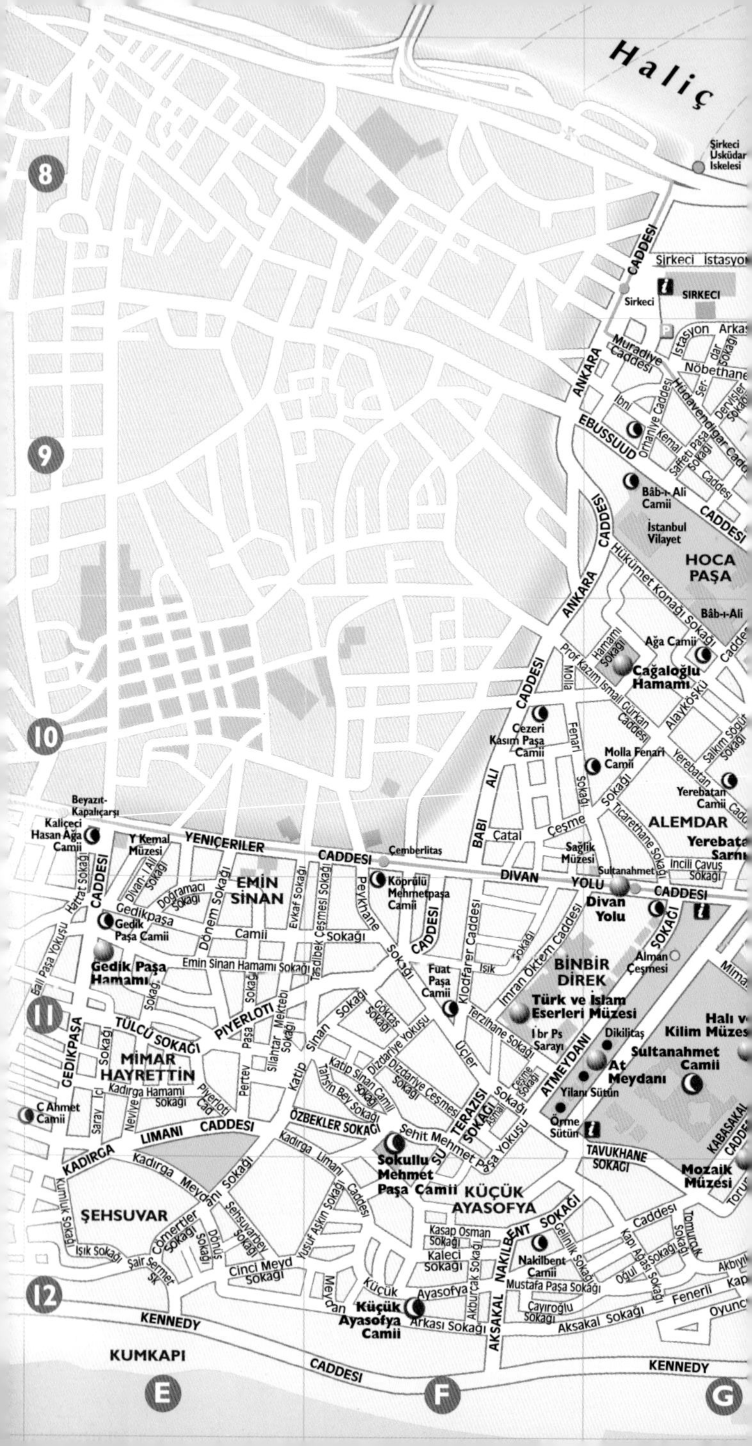
Haliç
Şirkeci Üsküdar İskelesi
CADDESİ
Şirkeci İstasyon
Sirkeci
SIRKECI
İstasyon Arka
Muradiye Caddesi
Ser-dar Sokağı
Nöbethane
ANKARA
İbni
Hüdavendigar Cad
Dervişler
EBUSSUUD
Orhaniye Caddesi
Kemal
Saffeti Paşa Sokağı
Caddesi
Bâb-ı-Ali Camii
CADDESİ
İstanbul Vilayet
HOCA PAŞA
Hükümet Konağı Sokağı
Bâb-ı-Ali
ANKARA
Ağa Camii
Hamamı Sokağı
Cağaloğlu Hamamı
Prof Kazım İsmail Gürkan Caddesi
Molla
Alayköşkü
CADDESİ
Cezeri Kasım Paşa Camii
Fenari Sokağı
Molla Fenari Camii
Salkım Söğüt
Yerebatan Sokağı
Yerebatan Camii
BABI ALİ
Çatal Çeşme
Sağlık Müzesi
Ticarethane Sokağı
ALEMDAR
Yerebatan Sarnı
Beyazıt-Kapalıçarşı
Kaliçeci Hasan Ağa Camii
Y Kemal Müzesi
YENİÇERİLER CADDESİ
Çemberlitaş
DIVAN YOLU CADDESİ
Sultanahmet
İncili Çavuş Sokağı
Divan-ı Ali Sokağı
Doğramacı Sokağı
EMİN SİNAN
Evkaf Sokağı
Tasdibek Çeşmesi Sokağı
Köprülü Mehmetpaşa Camii
Peykhane Sokağı
CADDESİ
Klodfarer Caddesi
Divan Yolu
SOKAĞI
Hattat Sokağı
CADDESİ
Gedikpaşa Camii
Gedik Paşa Camii
Dönem Sokağı
Emin Sinan Hamamı Sokağı
Işık
İmran Öktem Caddesi
BİNBİR DİREK
Alman Çeşmesi
Mimar
Sair Paşa Yokuşu
Gedik Paşa Hamamı
Sokağı
Fuat Paşa Camii
Türk ve İslam Eserleri Müzesi
Halı ve Kilim Müzesi
PİYERLOTİ
Paşa Sokağı
Mektebi Sokağı
Sinan Sokağı
Göktaş Sokağı
Terzihane Sokağı
İbr Ps Sarayı
Dikilitaş
GEDİKPAŞA
TÜLCÜ SOKAĞI
MİMAR HAYRETTİN
Pertev
Sıilantar
Katip
Dizdariye Yokuşu
Üçler
ATMEYDANI
At Meydanı
Sultanahmet Camii
Kadırga Hamamı Sokağı
Piyerloti Cad
Katip Sinan Camii Sokağı
Dizdariye Çeşmesi Sokağı
Çeşme Sokağı
Yılanlı Sütun
C Ahmet Camii
Saray İçi
Nevîye
Tahsin Bey Sokağı
TERAZISI SOKAĞI
SU
Sokağı
Örme Sütun
KADIRGA LİMANI CADDESİ
ÖZBEKLER SOKAĞI
Şehit Mehmet Paşa Yokuşu
TAVUKHANE SOKAĞI
KABASAKAL CADDESİ
Kadırga Limanı Caddesi
Sokullu Mehmet Paşa Camii
Mozaik Müzesi
Kadırga Meydanı Sokağı
KÜÇÜK AYASOFYA
Kumluk Sokağı
ŞEHSUVAR
Şehsuvarbey Sokağı
Yusuf Aşkın Sokağı
Cömertler Sokağı
Dönüş Sokağı
Kasap Osman Sokağı
NAKILBENT SOKAĞI
Nakilbent Camii
Gelinlik Sokağı
Caddesi
Kapı Ağası Sokağı
Tomurcuk Sokağı
Işık Sokağı
Şair Sermet SK
Cinci Meyd Sokağı
Kaleci Sokağı
Akburçak Sokağı
Mustafa Paşa Sokağı
Oğul Sokağı
Akbıyık
Küçük Ayasofya
Meydan
Küçük Ayasofya Camii
Arkası Sokağı
AKSAKAL
Çayıroğlu Sokağı
Aksakal Sokağı
Fenerli Kapı
Oyuncu
KENNEDY
KUMKAPI
CADDESİ
KENNEDY
8
9
10
11
12
E
F
G

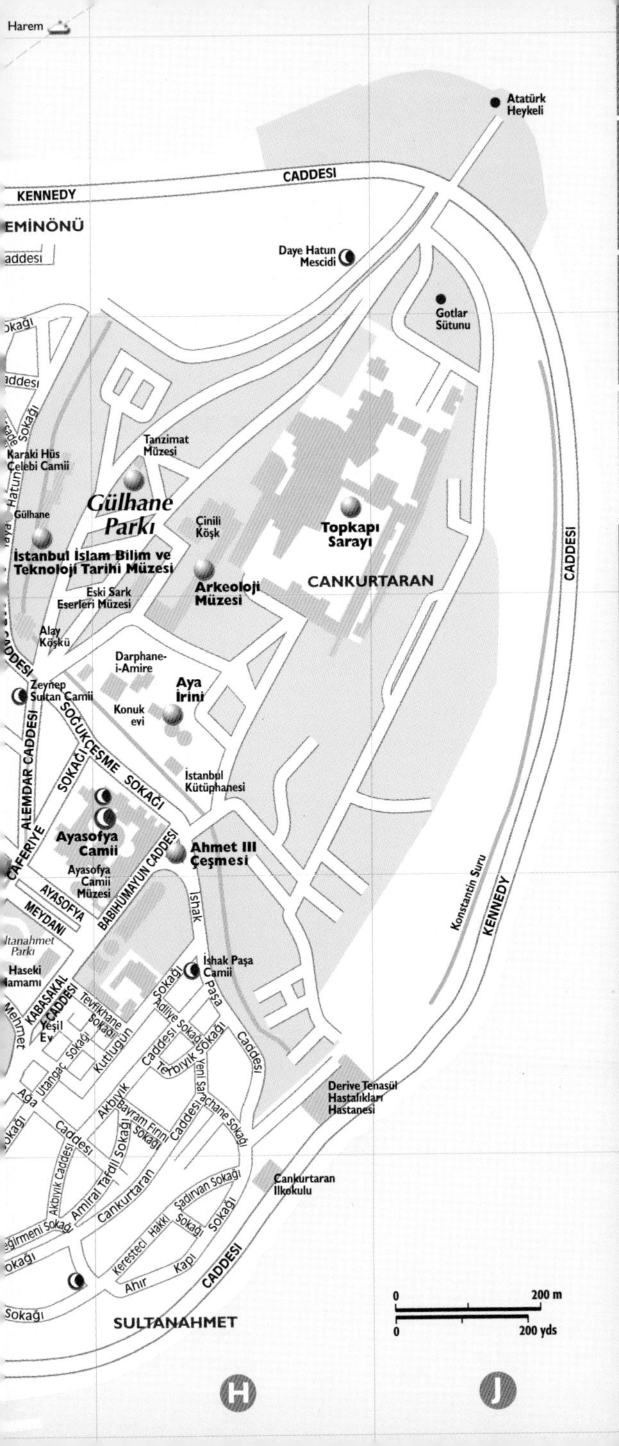
Harem
Atatürk Heykeli
KENNEDY
CADDESI
EMİNÖNÜ
Daye Hatun Mescidi
Gotlar Sütunu
Tanzimat Müzesi
Karaki Hüs Çelebi Camii
Gülhane
Gülhane Parkı
Çinili Köşk
Topkapı Sarayı
İstanbul İslam Bilim ve Teknoloji Tarihi Müzesi
Arkeoloji Müzesi
CANKURTARAN
Eski Sark Eserleri Müzesi
Alay Köşkü
Darphane-i-Amire
Aya İrini
Zeynep Sultan Camii
Konuk evi
SOĞUKÇEŞME SOKAĞI
ALEMDAR CADDESI
İstanbul Kütüphanesi
Ayasofya Camii
Ahmet III Çeşmesi
CAFERIYE
BABIHUMAYUN CADDESI
Ayasofya Camii Müzesi
AYASOFYA MEYDANI
İshak
İshak Paşa Camii
Haseki
KABASAKAL CADDESI
Tevfikhane Sokağı
Yeşil Ev
Adliye Sokağı
Utangaç Sokağı
Kutluğun
Caddesi
Terbıyık Sokağı
Yeni Saraçhane Sokağı
Akbıyık Caddesi
Bayram Fırını Sokağı
Amiral Tafdil Sokağı
Cankurtaran
Şadırvan Sokağı
Keresteci Hakkı Sokağı
Ahır Kapı Sokağı
Derive Tenasül Hastalıkları Hastanesi
Cankurtaran Ilkokulu
Konstantin Suru
SULTANAHMET
0
200 m
200 yds
H
J

Arkeoloji Müzesi

TOP 25

The Archaeological Museum contains some wonderful sculptures

THE BASICS

- H9
- Osman Hamdi Bey Yokuşu, Gülhane Parkı
- 212-520-7740
- Tue–Sun 9–5
- Garden café (€)
- Gülhane
- Few
- Inexpensive

HIGHLIGHTS

- Alexander sarcophagus
- Sarcophagus of the Mourning Women
- Lycian Sarcophagus
- Statue of Oceanus
- Bust of Emperor Augustus
- Phrygian alabaster perfume bottle in the shape of a goddess
- Gold earrings from Bronze Age Troy
- Fifth-century bc statue of wild boar from Edirne
- First-century BC sundial from Mesopotamia
- Treaty of Kadesh
- Tiled Kiosk of Sultan Mehmet the Conqueror

The Archaeological Museum's collections span 5,000 years. The star attraction is the Alexander sarcophagus, adorned with hunting and battle scenes of astonishing intensity.

Archaeological Museum Built to house the sarcophagi of the ancient Phoenician kings recovered by the archaeologist Osman Hamdi Bey in 1887, the museum also boasts a superb collection of classical sculptures. They include astonishingly lifelike busts of the Roman emperors, funerary stelae and a number of well-preserved statues. The new wing hosts a fascinating exhibition on the history of the area. Here you will find fragments of artwork preserved from lost Byzantine churches and a section of the defensive chain that hung across the Golden Horn in the 15th century.

Museum of the Ancient Orient Two 14th-century BC Hittite stone lions guard the entrance to this separate museum, which houses the oldest objects in the collection, including the sixth-century BC glazed-tile reliefs that lined the Processional Way into Babylon. There is a fabulous collection of cuneiform tablets—including the world's oldest peace accord, the Treaty of Kadesh, signed in the 13th century BC—together with law codes, judgements on murder and possibly the world's oldest love poem. The nearby Çinili Köşk (Tiled Pavilion) was built for Sultan Mehmet the Conqueror and is now a museum of ceramics from all over Turkey.

At Meydanı

The Egyptian Obelisk (left and middle); the Kaiser Wilhelm Fountain (right)

The most remarkable item in the Hippodrome is the Egyptian Obelisk, dating back to the 16th century BC. The hieroglyphs are so sharply etched that the column looks like a reproduction.

At Meydanı Originally a racecourse for charioteers, the Hippodrome was laid out on the site of the present park by the Emperor Septimius Severus in AD203 and enlarged by Constantine in the fourth century. The leading chariot teams, the Blues and the Greens, evolved into political factions and, in AD532, rioted against the Emperor Justinian, provoking General Belisarius to storm the Hippodrome, with the loss of 30,000 lives. The amphitheater, which could hold 100,000 people, was destroyed during the Fourth Crusade and the Ottomans plundered the ruins for the Sultanahmet Mosque. From the 16th century the square was known as At Meydanı (Horses' Square), after a polo-like game played here by the sultan's pages.

Monuments The racetrack was divided by a raised platform (*spina*), crowded with statues and monuments. Three of these survive, albeit in truncated form: the Egyptian Obelisk, commissioned by Pharaoh Thutmose III in the 16th century BC and brought to the city by Emperor Theodosius in AD390; the Serpent Column, imported by Constantine from the Temple of Apollo in Delphi (commemorating a 479BC victory over the Persians); and the 10th-century Column of Constantine Porphyrogenitus.

THE BASICS

G11
At Meydanı, Sultanahmet
Cafés around the edge (€)
Sultanahmet
None
Free

HIGHLIGHTS

- Kaiser Wilhelm Fountain
- Egyptian Obelisk
- Serpent Column
- Column of Constantine Porphyrogenitus
- Brick and stone facade of Ibrahim Paşa Sarayı (Museum of Turkish and Islamic Art, ▷ 36)
- Milion Taşı (First Milestone)
- View of Sultanahmet Mosque

Ayasofya Camii

TOP 25

HIGHLIGHTS

- Viking graffiti (Southern Gallery)
- Shafts of light through 40 windows of dome
- Carved capitals
- The Virgin and Christ flanked by Justinian and Constantine (mosaic in vestibule)
- Deisis mosaic in gallery
- 'Weeping column'
- Painting of angel mosaic, uncovered in 2009 (under dome)
- Sultan's Loge

Despite the peeling mosaics and crumbling masonry, this remains one of the world's architectural masterpieces. Insert your finger into the 'weeping column' in the nave—it is said to have miraculous healing powers.

History Ayasofya (or Haghia Sophia), the Church of Divine Wisdom, was commissioned by the Emperor Justinian in AD532. Despite its immense size—for a long time it was the largest religious building in the world—Ayasofya was completed in five years. Earthquakes nearly destroyed the building shortly afterwards, but despite this it remained the most important church in Christendom for nearly a thousand years. When Constantinople fell to the Turks in 1453, Sultan Mehmet II

Clockwise from far left: Marble pillars and ornate decoration inside Ayasofya Camii; the Deisis mosaic shows Christ flanked by John the Baptist and the Virgin Mary; the striking exterior; a vivid ceiling mosaic; an intricately carved capital; a mosaic showing the Virgin and Child

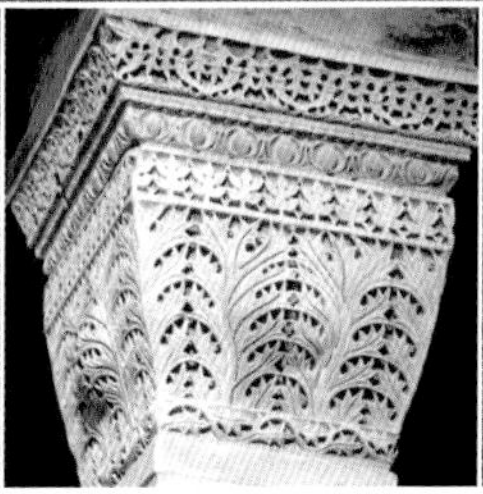

decreed the basilica should become a mosque. Since 1934 it has been the Ayasofya Museum.

Mosaics The walls and pillars of the basilica are patterned and decorated marble, brought from all over the known world: white marble from Marmara, purple porphyry from Egypt, verd antique from Thessaly and yellow marble from North Africa. But the chief glory of Ayasofya is its mosaics. There were originally more than 1.6ha (4 acres) of gold tesserae, and although a great deal has since disappeared you can still see some superb figurative mosaics, from the ninth to 13th centuries, in the Vestibule of the Warriors (narthex) and the galleries. There are portraits of emperors and an incomplete but arresting Deisis (Christ flanked by the Virgin Mary and John the Baptist).

THE BASICS

H10

Ayasofya Meydanı, Sultanahmet

212-522-0989/212-528-4500

Tue–Sun 9–5 (summer 9–7; winter 9–5)

Cafés (€), restaurants (€€) nearby

Sultanahmet

None

Moderate

Photography without flash allowed in museum

Küçük Ayasofya Camii

TOP 25

The mosque began life as a sixth-century church, commissioned by Emperor Justinian

THE BASICS

- F12
- Küçuk Ayasofya Caddesi
- Daily 9–7
- None
- Free/donation

HIGHLIGHTS

- Carved capitals on pillars
- Monogram of Justinian and Theodora on pillar
- Frieze celebrating Justinian, Theodora and Sergius (under gallery)
- Remains of sixth-century marble facings
- Irregular octagonal nave
- First-floor gallery

TIP

- Spend time relaxing in the charming courtyard, whose 16th-century *medrese* cells now house tea gardens, booksellers and artists' studios.

This pearl of a church, almost certainly the oldest in Istanbul, has an unusual octagonal design that has sometimes been put down to hurried workmanship but which adds to the building's charm.

Christian beginnings The 'Little' Ayasofya Mosque is even older than the great Byzantine church it resembles. It was commissioned by the Emperor Justinian in about AD527 from the architect Anthemius of Tralles, who also worked on Ayasofya. It was converted to a mosque early in the 16th century by the head of the Black Eunuchs, Hüseyin Ağa, who is buried in a tomb north of the apse. Damaged by earthquakes in 1648 and 1763, the mosque has now been restored to its former glory by the World Monuments Fund.

SS Sergius and Bacchus Emperor Justinian chose two martyred Roman soldiers, Sergius and Bacchus, to be patrons for his church. As a young man Justinian was accused of treason; it is said that Sergius and Bacchus had saved his life by appearing in a dream to the Emperor Anastasius and proclaiming his innocence.

A Byzantine survivor You'll find plenty of evidence of the mosque's earlier history, from the intricately carved decoration on the column capitals, some of which bear Justinian's monogram, to the traces of original gold leaf and marble that once adorned the church.

Fight between an elephant and a lion (left); a bearded man (right)

TOP 25

Mozaik Müzesi

One of the many remnants on view in the Mosaic Museum shows an elephant strangling a lion with its trunk—a scene that may have been acted out in the Belgrade Forest 15 centuries ago.

The palace The mosaics were discovered during excavations in the Arasta Bazaar in the 1930s and '50s. They are thought to date from the sixth century AD and to belong to the first imperial palace, begun in the reign of Constantine (AD324–37), which eventually stretched all the way from the Hippodrome to the sea walls.

The museum Little of the palace remains today apart from the ruined loggia at the entrance to the port and the superb mosaic friezes and pavements. These belonged to the peristyle (colonnade) of the Great Palace and would have been seen by the emperors when they retired to their private apartments. The cubes of glass, stone and terracotta radiate hues, while the action-packed scenes open a fascinating window onto everyday life in Byzantium. In one, a man falls from a donkey loaded with fruit; in another, a bear devours a young stag. There is a predilection for animal hunts, but there are more domestic scenes too: birds perching in a cypress tree, or two children riding on a camel. The most splendid image is of Dionysus, the Greek god of wine and fruitfulness, his luxuriant beard wreathed in green acanthus leaves.

THE BASICS

- G11
- Torun Sokağı, Sultanahmet
- 212-518-1205
- Tue–Sun 9–4.30 (summer 9–6)
- Cafés (€) and restaurants (€€) nearby
- None
- Inexpensive
- The marble window frames of the original palace are on the seafront at Kennedy Caddesi

HIGHLIGHTS

- Mosaic fragments in Arasta Bazaar
- Mosaics: man falling from donkey; camel ride; Dionysus tiger hunt; bear and stag; fight between an elephant and a lion

TIP

- To see more remains of Constantine's Great Palace, visit the museum at Eresin Crown hotel (▷ 110).

Sokullu Mehmet Paşa Camii

TOP 25

HIGHLIGHTS

- Tiled cap of *mimbar*
- Tiles on mihrab wall
- Pointed arches in courtyard
- Fragments from the Kaaba
- Lozenge capitals
- Arabesque paintings under gallery
- Ablution fountain
- Faïence panels above windows and doors

Istanbul's mosques are schools of religion as well as places of worship. In the courtyard of Sokullu Paşa you may hear the rhythmic hum of boys reciting the Koran, as they have done for centuries.

Sokullu Paşa This small masterpiece created by Mimar Sinan was commissioned by the Sultan's grand vizier, Sokullu Mehmet Paşa, in 1571–72. Born in Višegrad, Bosnia, in 1505, this formidable politician rose from falconer to viceroy of Europe before being appointed chief minister in 1565. His skills as a naval commander recommended him to Süleyman's successors and he achieved a notable victory in the capture of Tunis in 1574. Sokullu Paşa dedicated the mosque that bears his name to his wife, Ismihan Sultan, daughter of Selim II.

The Sokullu Mehmet Paşa Mosque, with its stunning tile decoration, dates from the 16th century

Interior The prayer hall of this well-proportioned building is a model of taste and refinement. Sinan planned it as a hexagon within a rectangle, the unusually high dome supported at the corners by four smaller semi-domes. A low gallery around three sides of the hall rests on slender marble columns with characteristic Ottoman lozenge capitals. The chief glory of the mosque is the mihrab wall, stunningly arrayed in tiles from the Iznik workshops. Swirling patterns of green and red tulips and carnations on a turquoise ground thrive in a visual context of pure white stone. Other treasures include some original painted arabesques under the gallery, fragments of black stone from the Kaaba in Mecca (above the entrance and in the mihrab wall) and the tiled crown on the *mimbar*, the only one of its kind in Istanbul.

THE BASICS

- F11
- Şehit Mehmet Paşa Sokak
- Daily 9–7
- None
- Free/donation

TIP

- If the mosque is closed, you can usually find a guardian to show you around in exchange for a donation.

Sultanahmet Camii

TOP 25

HIGHLIGHTS

- Blue Iznik tiles
- Six minarets
- Mausoleum of Sultan Ahmet I
- Inner courtyard

TIP

- Non-Muslim visitors should follow the signs to the entrance on the southern side, where you will be given a bag for your shoes and, if necessary, a shawl to cover bare shoulders and arms.

Better known to Western visitors as the 'Blue Mosque' because of the cobalt tiles in the prayer hall, this awesome building is particularly impressive when illuminated at night.

New mosque When Sultan Ahmet proposed building a new mosque in 1609, his advisers begged him to think again as the treasury was empty after a succession of failed military campaigns. But the sultan would have none of it and even insisted on digging the foundations himself. Sedefkar Mehmet Aša, a pupil of Mimar Sinan, designed the mosque, which was completed in 1616. It immediately became the focus of religious activities in the city—every Friday the sultan's procession would make its way from Topkapı Palace.

The Blue Mosque is an Istanbul landmark

Külliye The inner courtyard comprises an ornamental fountain and a most beautifully proportioned portico of 26 porphyry columns surmounted by 30 domes, while the view from above is of domes and semi-domes cascading from the mosque's summit in an apparently unbroken sequence.

Interior Inside, more than 20,000 Iznik tiles decorate the walls and galleries. Delicately painted with floral and geometrical designs, they are the work of a master craftsman, Çinici Hasan Usta. The stencils around the dome and the pillars are comparatively modern. Take a close look at the wooden doors and window frames, with their inlay of ivory, tortoiseshell and mother-of-pearl, and at the beautiful carving on the *mimbar* and the sultan's loge.

THE BASICS

www.bluemosque.com
G11
Sultanahmet Meydanı, Sultanahmet
212-518-1319
Daily 9–7; visitors' entrance open 8.30–12.30, 2–4.45, 5.45–6.30; closed Fri 12–2.30
Cafés (€) and restaurants (€€) nearby
Sultanahmet
Ramp
Free/donation

Topkapı Sarayı

TOP 25

HIGHLIGHTS

- Chinese and Japanese porcelain (kitchens)
- Divan
- Harem
- Relics of the Prophet Muhammad
- Sword of Mehmet the Conqueror
- Topkapı dagger

TIP

- Don't miss the Fourth Courtyard, with its views over the Bosphorus and Sea of Marmara.

The heartbeat of the Ottoman empire for nearly 400 years, Topkapı Palace is now a museum with extensive collections of imperial porcelain, jewels, costumes and arms.

The palace From 1461, when Mehmet II ordered its construction, to 1856, when the royal family moved to Dolmabahçe (▷ 96–97), Topkapı was both the sultan's private residence and the headquarters of the Ottoman empire. Allow half a day for a visit. You enter through the Imperial Gate, which leads to the First Courtyard, a public area where you will find Aya Irini church (▷ 38). You need to buy a ticket to enter the Second Courtyard, dominated by the Divan (Imperial Council Chamber), where the sultan's advisers met

Clockwise from far left: Visitors enter the palace; a bell backed by traditional blue tiles; view of the palace, surrounded by greenery; vivid tiling; gilded entrance to the Divan; a mosaic

to discuss matters of state while the sultan watched through a grille in the wall.

The Harem A separate ticket gives access to the Harem, the private quarters of the sultan and his family. This was a palace within a palace, with its own mosques, baths and 300 rooms in a labyrinth of corridors and courtyards, where the imperial wives and concubines were watched over by the valide sultan (queen mother). At the heart of the Harem is the Imperial Hall.

The Treasury The Third Courtyard contains the superb imperial treasures, from dazzling silk costumes to the emerald-studded Topkapı dagger and the revered sacred relics of the Prophet Muhammad.

THE BASICS

www.topkapisarayi.gov.tr
H9
Topkapı, Sultanahmet
212-512-0480
Wed–Mon 9–6. Harem: 9–5
Café (€), Konyalı restaurant (▷ 44)
Sultanahmet
Few
Expensive; separate charge for Harem
30-min guided tour of the Harem must be booked in advance to avoid a long wait

Türk ve Islam Eserleri Müzesi

TOP 25

See a fascinating selection of arts and crafts from the Islamic world

THE BASICS

F11
Ibrahim Paşa Sarayı, At Meydanı 46, Sultanahmet
212-518-1805
Tue–Sun 9–4.30 (summer 9–6)
Café (€)
Sultanahmet
None
Moderate

HIGHLIGHTS

- Audience Hall
- Carved lions and sphinxes
- Brass doorknobs depicting dragons from 12th-century mosque at Cizre
- Iznik tiles
- Engraved Selçuk drum
- Miniature Korans
- 'Holbein' carpet
- Brass lamps
- Yurt dwelling

TIP

- There are views of the Blue Mosque across the Hippodrome from the café terrace in the garden.

Have you ever wondered how the carpet came to be an indispensable item? Do you know how to make sheep's cheese? All is revealed in the Museum of Turkish and Islamic Art's ethnography section.

The palace The museum is housed in the former palace of Süleyman the Magnificent's grand vizier, Ibrahim Paşa, who received it as a gift from the sultan in 1520.

Arts and crafts The museum has an outstanding collection of arts and crafts from the Islamic world. You can see carved window shutters, gilded boxes, lacquered bookbindings and a relief map of the Ottoman empire in 1901.

Carpets Hanging in the former Audience Hall of the palace are carpets from as far afield as Hungary, Persia and Arab Spain, the earliest fragments dating back to the 13th century. Over time the paired birds, animals and tree motifs employed by the Seljuks gave way to more stylized geometrical patterns. This transition is recorded in Western art of the period, so it is appropriate that the designs themselves are named after the artists in whose paintings the carpets appear: Bellini, Van Eyck, Holbein.

Ethnography Carpet-weaving as a domestic handicraft originated with the nomadic peoples of Anatolia. Besides learning about natural dyes, you can visit a yurt, a black goatskin tent and other traditional dwellings.

One of two Medusa heads found here (left); some of the 336 columns (right)

TOP 25

Yerebatan Sarnıcı

The Basilica Cistern can easily be missed because it lies some 6m (19.5ft) below the ground, yet it is one of the most impressive sights in Istanbul. It dates back to AD532.

Imperial reservoir The cistern was built in the reign of the Emperor Justinian, primarily to supply water to the Great Palace. Aqueducts carried the water from its source in the Belgrade Forest, about 19km (12 miles) away. After the Ottoman conquest the cistern fell into disuse, although attempts were made to repair it in the 18th and 19th centuries. It was only in 1987, however, that this magnificent building was finally opened to the public.

Exploring the cistern Water still drips from the ceiling of the imposing, brick-vaulted chamber, although the strategically placed spotlights and specially constructed gangways make exploration easy. The main attraction—apart from the fish that thrive in the remaining several centimeters of water—is the forest of pillars supporting the magnificent arched roof. These columns are by no means uniform. Only about a third of the capitals are Corinthian, for example, while the patterning on one of the pillars resembles teardrops, on another peacock feathers. These inconsistencies suggest that they were removed from other sites and reused here, and might also account for the two Medusa heads found here, one set upside-down, the other lying on its side.

THE BASICS

www.yerebatan.com
G10
Yerebatan Caddesi, Sultanahmet
212-522-1259
Daily 9–8
Café (€)
Sultanahmet
None
Moderate
Occasional concerts and plays

HIGHLIGHTS

- Medusa heads
- 336 columns

TIP

- Look for classical concerts taking place in summer—this vast space has magnificent acoustics and the atmosphere of an underground cathedral.

More to See

AHMET III ÇEŞMESI

www.cagalogluhamami.com.tr

This rococo fountain, beside the Imperial Gate to Topkapı Palace (▷ 34–35), is the finest in Istanbul. One of many extravagances built for the Tulip Sultan, Ahmed III, its decoration is exuberant, with tinted marbles, floral reliefs and calligraphic patterning. The inscription reads 'Turn on the tap, drink the water and pray for the house of Ahmed.'

H10 Babıhümayun Caddesi, Sultanahmet Sultanahmet

AYA IRINI (CHURCH OF DIVINE PEACE)

This sturdy brick church is one of the oldest religious buildings in Istanbul. It was commissioned by Emperor Justinian in AD537, about the same time as Ayasofya (▷ 26–27). Of the once-lavish interior, only a mosaic of Christ on the Cross survives.

H10 First Courtyard, Topkapı Sarayı 212-528-4500 Cafés (€) nearby Gülhane Few Closed except for concerts (▷ 43)

CAĞALOĞLU HAMAMI

www.cagalogluhamami.com.tr

Opened in 1741, in the reign of Mahmut I, these baths are probably the most famous in Istanbul, with a guest list that claims to include Franz Liszt, Florence Nightingale and Cameron Diaz. Treatments range from a self-service bath to a body scrub, shampoo and massage 'fit for a sultan'.

G10 Kazım Ismail Gürkan Caddesi 34, Sultanahmet 212-522-2424 Daily 8am–10pm for men; 8–8 for women Sultanahmet

DIVAN YOLU

Crowded with cafés, restaurants and retail outlets, this was once the main street of Byzantium, known as the Mese (Middle Way). Centuries later it became Divan Yolu (Road of the Divan Council), the traditional Ottoman processional route from the city to Topkapı Palace.

G11 Divan Yolu, Sultanahmet Cafés (€) and restaurants (€€) Sultanahmet, Çemberlitaş

The Ahmet III Fountain dates from 1726

The Church of Divine Peace

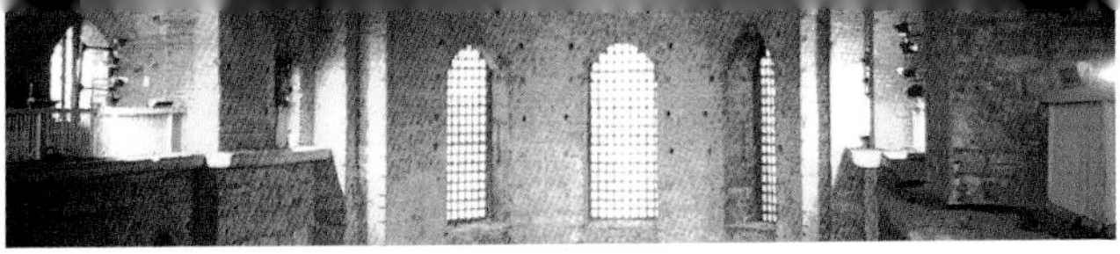

GEDIK PAŞA HAMAMI

www.gedikpasahamami.com

Dating from 1475, soon after the Ottoman conquest, these baths may well be the oldest in the city. The founder, Gedik Ahmet Paşa, was grand vizier under Mehmet the Conqueror and commander of the Ottoman fleet. The hammam is capped by an impressive dome and flanked by alcoves and cubicles faced with marble.

E11 Emin Sinan Hamamı Sokağı, Sultanahmet 212-517-8956 Daily 6am–midnight Beyazıt

GÜLHANE PARKI

This wooded park in the heart of Sultanahmet was created from the old rose garden of Topkapı Palace (▷ 34–35). Apart from the views of the Bosphorus and the statue of Atatürk, you can admire the Alay Köşkü (Review Pavilion), which is built into the wall by the main gate.

H9 Alemdar Caddesi Daily Cafés; Set Üstü (▷ 43) Gülhane

HALI VE KILIM MÜZESI

This fabulous collection of ancient carpets and kilims is administered by the General Directorate of Pious Foundations and housed within the precincts of the Blue Mosque (▷ 32–33), in the recently restored Imperial Pavilion once used by visiting sultans for prayer.

G11 Sultanahmet Camii 212-518-1330 Tue–Sat 9–12, 1–4 Cafés and restaurants (€€) nearby Sultanahmet None Inexpensive

ISTANBUL ISLAM BILIM VE TEKNOLOJI TARIHI MÜZESI

This unusual museum opened in 2008 in the former royal stables in Gülhane Park and focuses on the role of the Islamic world in the development of science and technology. The exhibits, which include water clocks and medical instruments, are replicas based on contemporary Arab drawings and manuscripts.

G9 Has Ahırlar Binaları, Gülhane Parkı 212-528-8065 Wed–Mon 9–6.30 Gülhane Inexpensive

Taking a break in Gülhane Parkı

Sultanahmet Walk

Take in the main sights of Sultanahmet on a historical stroll through Ottoman Istanbul.

DISTANCE: 2.5km (1.5 miles) **ALLOW:** 1 hour

START

AT MEYDANI (▷ 25)
G11 Sultanahmet

❶ Start in At Meydani (the Hippodrome, ▷ 25), with your back to the Blue Mosque. Turn left past the Obelisk and Serpent Column. Head for Şehit Mehmet Paşa Yokuşu, a cobbled street in the corner of the square.

❷ Follow this street as it bends right and heads sharply downhill. Keep straight ahead at a crossroads past Hotel Daphne, passing Sokullu Mehmet Paşa Camii (▷ 30–31) on your left before reaching Kadirga Limani Caddesi.

❸ Turn left then right into Kuçuk Ayasofya Camii Sokağı. When you reach the mosque (▷ 28), turn left into Kuçuk Ayasofya Caddesi and stay on this street as it climbs towards the Blue Mosque.

❹ Keep right to walk through the Arasta Bazaar (▷ 42). At the end of the bazaar, climb the steps, turn left then right along Kabasakal Caddesi.

❺ Continue along Babıhümayun Caddesi until you reach the Imperial Gate at the entrance to Topkapı Palace (▷ 34–35), with the magnificent Ahmed III Fountain on your right.

❻ Turn left along Soğukçeşme Sokağı, where an entire row of Ottoman wooden houses has been converted into a hotel beside the palace walls.

❼ Turn left on Caferiye Sokağı, arriving on Ayasofya Meydanı near the entrance to Ayasofya Camii (▷ 26–27).

❽ Cross the square to reach the park with a fountain at the heart between the Blue Mosque and Ayasofya. Continue through the precincts of the Blue Mosque (▷ 32–33; pictured left) to return to the Hippodrome.

END

AT MEYDANI (▷ 25)
G11 Sultanahmet

Shopping

ARASTA ÇARŞISI
www.arastabazaar.com
A miniature, more relaxed version of the Grand Bazaar, the Arasta Bazaar has 40 shops selling carpets, jewelry and pottery in the old Ottoman stables beside the Blue Mosque. Unlike the Grand Bazaar, it is open on Sunday.
G11–12 Arasta Çarşısı, Sultanahmet
Sultanahmet

COCOON
www.cocoontr.com
You cannot miss this store, with its wacky display of felt hats, rugs, antique costumes and textiles from all over central Asia taking up most of the window.
G12 Küçük Ayasofya Caddesi 13, Sultanahmet
212-638-6450
Sultanahmet

DÖSIM BKG
The new museum shop in the grounds of Topkapi Palace sells a wide range of desirable handicrafts and souvenirs, including porcelain, silk scarves, commemorative mugs, tea glasses, Turkish delight, maps and guides.
H10 First Courtyard, Topkapı Sarayı 212-513-0480 Sultanahmet

ELEGANCE
www.elegancecarpet.com
This smart showroom just off the Hippodrome has wool and silk carpets and kilims from the city of Kayseri, in central Turkey. Prices are not low but staff are knowledgeable and friendly.
G10 Yerebatan Caddesi 46–48, Sultanahmet
212-511-7527
Sultanahmet

GALERI CENGIZ
This shop in the Arasta Çarşısı (▷ this page) has old and new carpets and kilims, as well as accessories made out of kilim material.
G11 Arasta Çarşısı 155–157, Sultanahmet
212-518-8882
Sultanahmet

GALERI KAYSERI
www.galerikayseri.com
With two shops facing each other near the foot of Divan Yolu, Galeri Kayseri offers Sultanahmet's best selection of English-language books about Turkey and Istanbul.
G11 Divan Yolu Caddesi 11 and 58 212-512-0456 Sultanahmet

KNOW YOUR CARPETS

First, remember that kilims are woven and have don't have any pile, while carpets are knotted. Second, ask the dealer whether or not the dyes are natural or synthetic (natural last longer). Third, inspect the tightness of the weave (the greater the number of knots, the more expensive the carpet). Finally, take advice but don't be browbeaten—take your time and find the right one. Choose the pattern and shades that appeal to you most—after all, it is you who has to live with the carpet.

ISTANBUL HANDICRAFTS CENTRE
Watch the artists at work in this courtyard bazaar, in an 18th-century *medrese* (religious school) beside the Yeşil Ev hotel. Among the items produced and sold here are calligraphy, glassware, ceramics, Turkish dolls and miniature paintings.
G11 Kabasakal Caddesi 11, Sultanahmet
212-517 6782
Sultanahmet

IZNIK TILES
www.iznikclassics.com
Beautiful hand-painted ceramic tiles and plates, sold from two shops in the Arasta Çarşısı.
G11 Arasta Çarşısı 67, Sultanahmet 212-517-1705 Sultanahmet

STEEL LEATHER
A wide range of competitively priced, off-the-peg leather jackets and coats for sale. Or work to your own specifications can be turned out within 24 hours by this English-speaking tailor.
G10 Incili Çavuş Ateş Pasajı 33/13, Sultanahmet
212-513-7794
Sultanahmet

Entertainment and Nightlife

AKBIYIK CADDESI
Especially popular with back-packers, this lively street of late-night bars, cafés and restaurants offers food and drink at bargain basement prices and loud disco music. Bustling but quieter during daylight hours.
H11 Akbıyık Caddesi, Cankurtaran Sultanahmet

AYA IRINI
This beautiful sixth-century church (Church of Divine Peace (▷ 38) is open for concerts during the annual International Music Festival (June and July).
H10 First Courtyard, Topkapı Sarayı 212-528-4500 Only for concerts Gülhane

CAFÉ MEŞALE
Set in a sunken courtyard in the shadow of the Blue Mosque, this attractive outdoor café has cushions, rugs and low stools where you can make yourself comfortable and listen to live folk music or watch dervish dancing displays most evenings. In common with other tea gardens, it serves Turkish tea, coffee and waterpipes but not alcohol.
G11 Arasta Çarşısı 45, Sultanahmet 212-518-9562 Daily 24 hours Sultanahmet

CAĞALOĞLU HAMAMI
See page 38.

DERVIŞ AILE CAY BAHÇESI
Delightful tea garden opposite the Blue Mosque, with whirling dervish performances every night in summer.
G11 Kabasakal Caddesi 1, Sultanahmet No phone Daily 9am–11pm Sultanahmet

GEDIK PAŞA HAMAMI
See page 39.

HAVUZBAŞI
This sunken tea garden is a delightful place with its fountain and views of the Blue Mosque. There's also live Turkish folk music every night in summer.
F12 Nakilbent Sokağı 2, Sultanahmet 212-638-8819 Daily 10am–midnight

WHAT'S ON

There's huge range of live events to enjoy throughout the year, so to find out what's on while you're in Istanbul, pick up a copy of the monthly *Time Out Istanbul*, which is published in Turkish- and English-language editions. The easiest way of getting tickets is from the box office of the various venues, but tickets for arts and sports events are also available through Biletix (216-556-9800; www.biletix.com). Biletix has ticket outlets throughout the city, including Vakkorama in the Akmerkez shopping mall (▷ 104) and at the Istiklâl Kitabevi bookshop, found at Istiklâl Caddesi (▷ 80–81).

THE NORTH SHIELD PUB
This friendly sports bar, located right by the tram stop on Divan Yolu, serves draught beer and good pub grub, including steaks. Prices are on the steep side but there's a great vibe on match days and it's a wonderful place to soak up the local atmosphere and get to know Turkish sports' fans.
G9 Alemdar Caddesi 1, Sultanahmet Daily 10am–2pm Gülhane

SET ÜSTÜ
Tea is served in brass pots, and there are fabulous views over Seraglio Point and the Bosphorus from this peaceful tea garden near the Kennedy Caddesi entrance to Gülhane Park.
J8 Gülhane Parkı Daily 9–9 Gülhane

YENI MARMARA
A traditional and relaxing café set on a summer terrace, overlooking the Sea of Marmara, where many local people like to come to meet friends, sip Turkish coffee, play backgammon and smoke waterpipes.
G12 Çayiroğlu Sokağı, Sultanahmet 212-516-9013 Daily 8am–midnight Sultanahmet

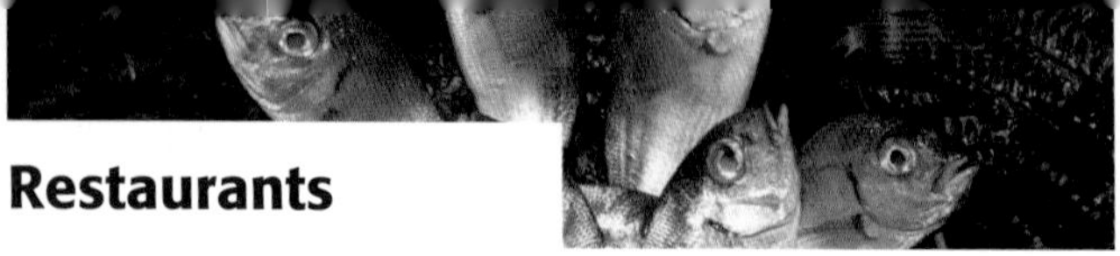

Restaurants

PRICES

Prices are approximate, based on a three-course meal for one person.

€€€	over 50 TL
€€	30–50 TL
€	under 30 TL

ALORAN (€€)
A deservedly popular Turkish restaurant serving well-prepared, good-value succulent stews, kebabs and fish dishes. Cheerful and courteous service. Due to its popularity, terrace reservations advised.
H11 Adiye Sokak 11, Cankurtaran 212-458-8528 Daily 9am–midnight Sultanahmet

BEYAZ (€€€)
Unlike most restaurants in Kumkapı, this is right on the port, with views across the Sea of Marmara, and fresh fish from the nearby market.
D12 Balıkcılar Çarşısı 28, Kennedy Caddesi, Kumkapı 212-518-3631 Daily 12–12 Kumkapı

CENNET (€)
Anatolian women in traditional dress prepare delicious lava bread pancakes (*gözleme*) in this folksy eaterie. Meat or vegetable fillings and a large choice of well-prepared appetizers are also available.
F10 Binbirdirek Mh, Divanyolu Caddesi 31/A, Çemberlitaş 212-518-8111 Daily 8am–11pm Çemberlitaş

DOY-DOY (€€)
www.doydoy-restaurant.com
Filling menu of kebabs, salad, *lahmacun* (Turkish pizza) and grilled fish in the backstreets, downhill from the Hippodrome. There's a view of the Blue Mosque from the rooftop terrace.
G12 Şifa Hamamı Sokağı 13, Sultanahmet 212-517-1588 Daily 9am–11pm Sultanahmet

KONYALı (€€)
The attraction here is the setting, in the grounds of Topkapı Palace with views over the Bosphorus. Get here early for the Turkish cuisine, before the tour parties arrive.
J9 Fourth Courtyard, Topkapı Sarayı 212-513-9696 Wed–Mon 10–5 Sultanahmet

KUMKAPI

The ancient port of Kumkapı has the highest concentration of seafood restaurants in Istanbul—well over 50, mostly crowded around the main square. There are spectacular views of the Marmara from the fish market on Kennedy Caddesi, but if it's atmosphere you're after, head inland behind the railway station, where tables spill out onto the street and musicians serenade you while you dine. With its atmospheric twinkling lights, flower sellers, bubbling fountains and cobbled streets, Kumkapı buzzes on summer evenings.

RAMI (€€€)
www.ramirestaurant.com
Contemporary Ottoman cuisine in a restored wooden house, with fabulous views of the Blue Mosque from the rooftop terrace.
G11 Utangaç Sokağı 6 212-517-6593 Daily 12–12 Sultanahmet

SARNIÇ (€€€)
www.sarnicrestaurant.com
High-class Turkish cuisine in a converted Roman cistern behind Ayasofya is highly atmospheric when lit by candles at night.
H10 Soğukçeşme Sokağı 6 212-512-4291 Daily 7pm–11pm Gülhane

TARIHI SULTANAHMET KÖFTECISI (€)
www.sultanahmetkofteccisi.com
Opened in 1920 and still serving the same no-nonsense menu of *köfte* (meatballs), kebabs, salads, beans and rice to crowds of satisfied customers.
G11 Divan Yolu Caddesi 12, Sultanahmet 212-520-0566 Daily 12–10 Sultanahmet

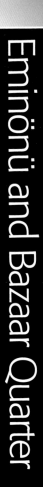

Eminönü and Bazaar Quarter

With hawkers selling inexpensive goods by the quayside and ferries chugging across the mouth of the Golden Horn, Eminönü marks the start of the sprawling Bazaar Quarter, where steep streets climb the slopes to the labyrinthine Grand Bazaar.

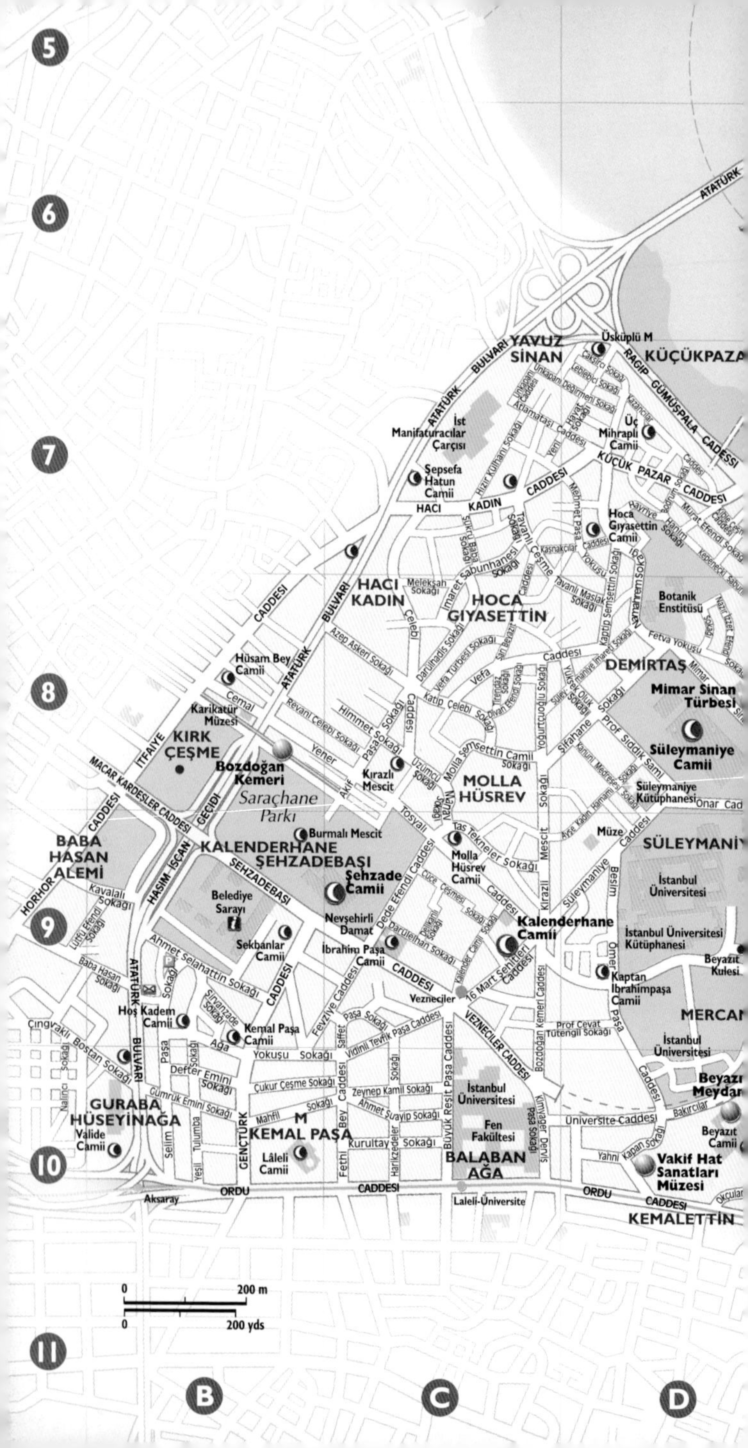
5
6
7
8
9
10
11
B
C
D
ATATÜRK
YAVUZ SİNAN
Üsküplü M
KÜÇÜKPAZA
RAGIP GÜMÜŞPALA CADDESİ
ATATÜRK BULVARI
İst Manifaturacılar Çarşısı
Üç Mihraplı Camii
Şepsefa Hatun Camii
KÜÇÜK PAZAR CADDESİ
HACI KADIN CADDESİ
Hoca Gıyasettin Camii
HACI KADIN
HOCA GIYASETTİN
Botanik Enstitüsü
Fetva Yokuşu
DEMİRTAŞ
Mimar Sinan Türbesi
Süleymaniye Camii
Hüsam Bey Camii
Karikatür Müzesi
KIRK ÇEŞME
Bozdoğan Kemeri
Saraçhane Parkı
Kırazlı Mescit
MOLLA HÜSREV
Süleymaniye Kütüphanesi
Onar Cad
Müze
SÜLEYMANİY
MACAR KARDESLER CADDESİ
İTFAİYE
GEÇİDİ
Burmalı Mescit
BABA HASAN ALEMİ
KALENDERHANE
ŞEHZADEBAŞI
Şehzade Camii
Molla Hüsrev Camii
İstanbul Üniversitesi
HORHOR CADDESİ
HASIM İŞCAN
ŞEHZADEBAŞI
Belediye Sarayı
Nevşehirli Damat
Kalenderhane Camii
İstanbul Üniversitesi Kütüphanesi
Beyazıt Kulesi
Sekbanlar Camii
İbrahim Paşa Camii
Kaptan İbrahimpaşa Camii
Vezneciler
16 Mart Şehitleri Caddesi
VEZNECİLER CADDESİ
MERCAN
Hoş Kadem Camii
Kemal Paşa Camii
ATATÜRK BULVARI
Prof Cevat Tütengil Sokağı
İstanbul Üniversitesi
Beyazıt Meydan
GURABA HÜSEYİNAĞA
Valide Camii
İstanbul Üniversitesi
Fen Fakültesi
Üniversite Caddesi
Bakırcılar
Beyazıt Camii
M KEMAL PAŞA
Lâleli Camii
BALABAN AĞA
Vakif Hat Sanatları Müzesi
Aksaray
ORDU CADDESİ
Laleli-Üniversite
ORDU CADDESİ
KEMALETTİN
0
200 m
0
200 yds

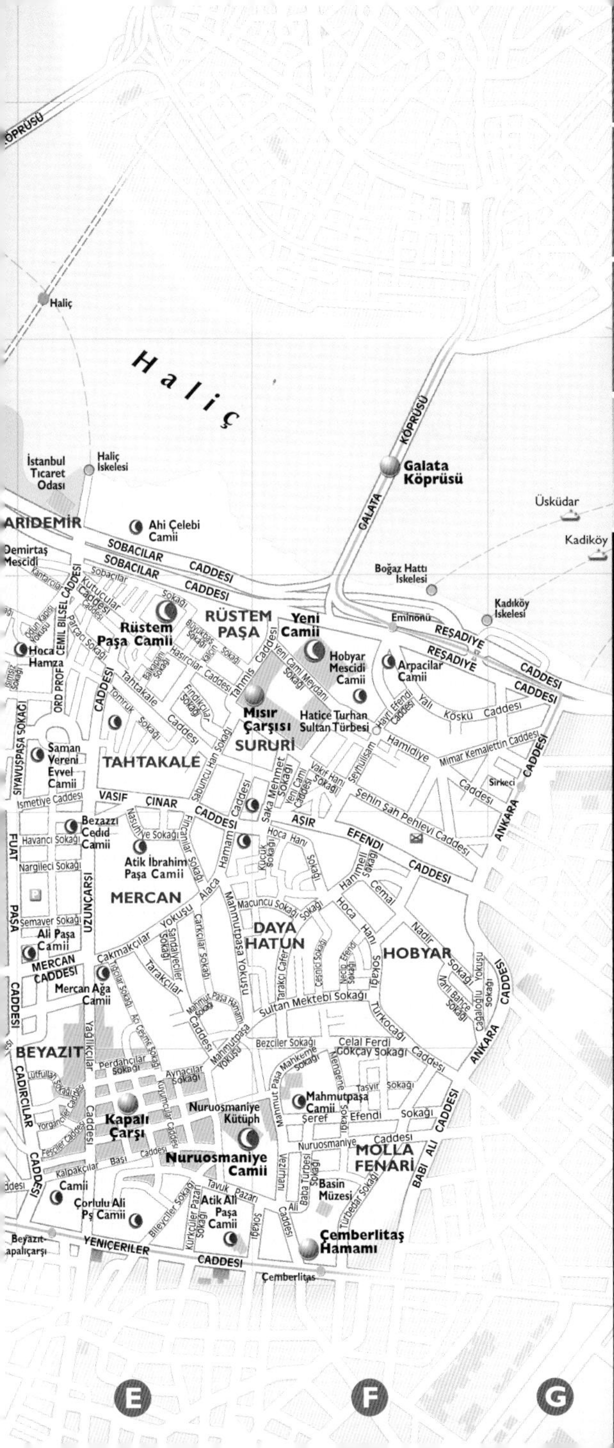
Haliç
Haliç
İstanbul Ticaret Odası
Haliç İskelesi
Galata Köprüsü
GALATA KÖPRÜSÜ
Üsküdar
Kadıköy
Boğaz Hattı İskelesi
Kadıköy İskelesi
Eminönü
ARIDEMİR
Ahi Çelebi Camii
Demirtaş Mescidi
SOBACILAR CADDESİ
SOBACILAR CADDESİ
RÜSTEM PAŞA
Yeni Camii
Rüstem Paşa Camii
Hoca Hamza
Hobyar Mescidi Camii
Arpacilar Camii
REŞADİYE CADDESİ
REŞADİYE CADDESİ
CEMİL BİLSEL CADDESİ
ORD PROF
Mısır Çarşısı
Hatice Turhan Sultan Türbesi
SURURİ
TAHTAKALE
Saman Vereni Evvel Camii
SİYAVUŞPAŞA SOKAĞI
Yalı Köşkü Caddesi
Hamidiye Caddesi
Mimar Kemalettin Caddesi
Sirkeci
ANKARA CADDESİ
Şehin Şah Pehlevi Caddesi
VASIF ÇINAR CADDESİ
AŞIR EFENDİ CADDESİ
İsmetiye Caddesi
Bezazzi Cedid Camii
Atik İbrahim Paşa Camii
FUAT PAŞA
MERCAN
DAYA HATUN
HOBYAR
Ali Paşa Camii
MERCAN CADDESİ
Mercan Ağa Camii
UZUNÇARŞI
Mahmutpaşa Yokuşu
Sultan Mektebi Sokağı
BEYAZIT
ÇADIRCILAR CADDESİ
Kapalı Çarşı
Nuruosmaniye Kütüph
Nuruosmaniye Camii
Mahmutpaşa Camii
MOLLA FENARİ
BABI ALİ CADDESİ
Basin Müzesi
Çorlulu Ali Pş Camii
Atik Ali Paşa Camii
Çemberlitaş Hamamı
YENİÇERİLER CADDESİ
Beyazıt-Kapalıçarşı
Çemberlitaş
E
F
G

Beyazıt Meydanı

TOP 25

Street vendor (left); the mausoleum (middle); shoppers with their purchase (right)

THE BASICS

- D10
- Beyazıt Meydanı
- Lively café scene in nearby streets
- Beyazıt

HIGHLIGHTS

- University Gate (Calligraphy Museum, ▷ 57)
- Forum Taurii ruins
- Mosque courtyard

TIP

- A lane behind the mosque contains the Sahaflar Çarşısı (Booksellers' Bazaar), where books have been traded since Ottoman times. Students from the nearby university come here to buy textbooks and there are stalls selling framed calligraphy and antique coins.

This large open square on the site of the Roman forum is a great place to take the pulse of the city.

The square Beyazıt Meydanı, one of Istanbul's busiest squares, occupies the site of the Forum Taurii, once a thriving Byzantine market-place–you can see some remains of it on the other side of Ordu Caddesi, part of the Roman street known as the Mese. Today the square contains the ceremonial gateway to Istanbul University and the Beyazıt Mosque medrese, now the Calligraphy Museum.

The mosque The graceful Beyazıt Mosque was built between 1501 and 1506 in the reign of Beyazıt II, making it the oldest surviving Ottoman mosque in Istanbul. You will find Beyazıt's *türbe* (mausoleum) in the cemetery behind the mosque. The architect of this magnificent complex, Yakub Şah, clearly had an eye for detail as well as an instinct for geometrical proportion. He used these gifts to brilliant effect in the colonnaded courtyard, where the columns of contrasting red, gray and green marble are crowned with stalactite decoration. Yakub Şah based the interior on the Christian church of Ayasofya. Four massive piers support the central dome, which is flanked by two semi-domes. The *mimbar* (staircase), mihrab and beautifully sculptured balustrade are original 16th-century features, as is the sultan's loge, to the right of the *mimbar*, which rests on columns of precious marble.

Treat yourself to a Turkish bath or massage

TOP 25 Çemberlitaş Hamamı

This magnificent bathhouse is the best place to initiate yourself into the delights of the Turkish bath.

The baths The baths were founded in 1584 by Valide Sultan Nurbanu, the widow of Sultan Selim II, and have been in continuous use ever since. Designed by architect Mimar Sinan, they remain one of the finest examples of 16th-century Ottoman civil architecture in Istanbul. The baths are divided into the traditional male and female sections, with marble alcoves and washbasins around a central *hararet* (steam room), where sunlight filters in through star-shaped skylights in the dome.

Beginner's guide On arrival, you will be shown into the *camekan*, a courtyard with wooden cubicles around the edge, where you should undress and leave your clothes. The attendant will give you a *peştemal*, a cotton towel, to wrap around your body, and a pair of slippers. You pass through the *soğukluk* (cool room) on your way to the *hararet*, where you lie and sweat for about 15 minutes on a heated marble platform known as a *göbek taşı* (navel stone). If you have chosen the massage, an attendant will then pummel and knead your body, scrub your skin with a coarse *kese* (mitten) and wash you all over with soap. Afterwards, you are free to relax in the *hararet* (steam room) for as long as you like before returning to the *camekan* to collect your clothes.

THE BASICS

www.cemberlitashamami.com.tr
- F10
- Vezirhanı Caddesi 8
- 212-522-7974
- Daily 6am–midnight
- Çemberlitaş
- Expensive

TIPS

- You can choose between a self-service bath and a massage. Both are enjoyable, but for the full hammam experience, it is worth paying extra for the massage at least once.
- Take plenty of change as the masseurs and cloakroom attendants will all expect a tip.

Kapalı Çarşı

TOP 25

HIGHLIGHTS

- Iç Bedesten
- Zincirli Han
- Mosques, baths and fountains

TIPS

- Visit on Wednesday at 1pm, when a carpet auction takes place in the Sandal Bedesten.
- Prices are not fixed and the traders are skilled at bargaining, so you need patience and good humor to negotiate a purchase.

The Covered Bazaar, usually referred to as the Grand Bazaar, was built after the Ottoman conquest as the city's main market—making it perhaps the world's oldest shopping mall.

Iç Bedesten The bazaar is a labyrinth of seemingly endless vaulted arcades and passageways lined with merchants selling their wares—a city within a city. At the heart of the market is the Iç Bedesten, which dates from the period of the Ottoman conquest (1456–61). An enormous warehouse surrounded by market stalls and workshops, it was once covered by canvas awnings. Today it deals in Ottoman antiques.

Orientation Traditionally, certain streets specialize in the sale of particular items—Halıcılar

There's plenty to buy at the Grand Bazaar, from carpets and brassware to traditional tiles and eye-catching slippers

Caddesi, for example, means 'Carpet-Sellers' Street'. If you are looking for leatherware, head for Keseciler Caddesi; if it's gold and silverware you are after, try Kalpakçılar Caddesi. The range of goods is astonishing: hand-painted bowls, brass lamps, embroidered waistcoats, T-shirts, kilim bags, meerschaum pipes, Iznik tiles and the ubiquitous amulets to ward off the 'evil eye'. Shopping in the bazaar can be tiring, but there are many cafés where you can join the traders taking tea or enjoying a game of backgammon.

Hans Don't leave the bazaar without taking a detour into the picturesque courtyards of the old *hans* or caravanserais, built originally to accommodate merchants. The ground floors of these arcaded buildings, once stables and storerooms, are now used as workshops.

THE BASICS

www.grandbazaaristanbul.org
E10
Kapalı Çarşı, Beyazıt
Mon–Sat 9–7
Restaurants (€€) and cafés (€)
Tram to Çemberlitaş or Beyazıt
None
Free

Mısır Çarşısı

TOP 25

Enjoy the aroma of herbs and spices as you shop in the Spice Bazaar

THE BASICS

- F8
- Yeni Camii Meydanı, Eminönü
- Mon–Sat 9–7
- Pandeli restaurant (lunch only; ▷ 62)
- Eminönü
- Eminönü
- None
- Free

HIGHLIGHTS

- Pistachio-filled Turkish delight
- Honeycomb
- Saffron
- Caviar from Azerbaijan
- Nuts and dried fruit
- Brass pepper mills

TIP

- Take time to explore the streets around the bazaar, with their delicatessens, coffee shops and fresh produce markets.

The Spice Bazaar makes for a more relaxing shopping trip than the Grand Bazaar because it's easier to find your way around. See how much Turkish delight you can sample before having to buy some.

Egyptian Bazaar Completed in 1663 for Turhan Hatice Sultan, mother of Mehmet IV, the Spice Bazaar was intended to provide income for the charitable foundations of the nearby Yeni Mosque (▷ 57). The source of this income was the import duties levied on the spices as they passed through Egypt (which was at that time part of the Ottoman empire), which is why the Turks still call this the Egyptian Bazaar.

Turkish delight The entrance to the bazaar is through one of four robust, double-arched gates. Of the shops here today, only a few specialize exclusively in herbs and spices; even so, the aroma is unmistakable, a heady mix of saffron, coriander, ginger, cinnamon, paprika, sage and tamarind. The second overwhelming impression is the riot of color. You will see hanging aubergines (eggplants), paprika and salamis, trays filled with sweets, nuts, dried figs and apricots, and counters stacked with red, yellow, blue and green pots of caviar. Few can resist the Turkish delight, with its hazelnut and pistachio fillings; or the tea, scented with apples, oranges, lemons, cherries, cinnamon and rose hip.

Richly decorated Iznik tiles line the walls of the Rüstem Paşa Mosque

TOP 25

Rüstem Paşa Camii

This is the best place in Istanbul to learn to love the tile-maker's art. If you can, visit the gallery, where you will find examples of the architect Mimar Sinan's original designs, which were considered too restrained by Rüstem Paşa.

The mosque This little gem of a mosque dates from 1561. It was designed by Sinan for Süleyman the Magnificent's son-in-law, Grand Vizier Rüstem Paşa, although he never lived to see it completed. The charitable institutions of the *külliye* were financed by the vaulted shops that Sinan constructed at street level below the expansive terrace leading to the mosque itself. Space was at a premium in the city's commercial quarter, so the courtyard area is restricted to a highly unusual double porch. The sloping roof is supported by a row of delicately carved stone pillars.

Decoration Sinan planned the prayer hall as an octagon inscribed within a rectangle. The main dome is flanked by four semi-domes, one at each corner of the building, and rests on four massive octagonal columns and four pillars abutting on the east and west walls. There are galleries on the north and south sides. Following Rüstem Paşa's death, his widow, Mihrimah Sultan, spared no expense on the decoration of the mosque. Every available space is set with exquisite Iznik tiles, designed by artists at the palace's own workshops and featuring extravagant geometric and floral motifs.

THE BASICS

- E8
- Hasırcılar Caddesi, Eminönü
- Daily 9–7
- Cafés (€) nearby
- Eminönü
- Eminönü
- None
- Free/donation

HIGHLIGHTS

- Terrace
- Double porch
- Carved stone capitals (porch)
- Lozenge capitals (prayer hall)
- Dome
- Iznik tiles
- Octagonal columns
- Calligraphic shields under dome

TIP

- Keep your eyes peeled for the entrances to the Mosque, up the steps between the shop fronts.

Süleymaniye Camii

TOP 25

HIGHLIGHTS

- Four minarets with 10 balconies, symbolizing Süleyman's position as the fourth sultan after the Conquest, and the tenth Ottoman sultan overall
- *Medreses*
- Dome of mosque
- Iznik tiles on mihrab wall
- Mausoleum of Süleyman the Magnificent
- Mausoleum of Haseki Hürrem Sultan

Mimar Sinan's masterpiece was built for his patron, Süleyman the Magnificent, who is buried in a mausoleum in the garden alongside his wife Haseki Hürrem, better known as Roxelana.

Külliye With the construction of the Süleymaniye Mosque complex between 1550 and 1559, the architect Sinan finally emancipated himself from the influence of Ayasofya to reveal his astonishing originality. In the 16th century the entire compound would have hummed with activity—within its precincts were four *medreses*, schools, kitchens, shops, baths and a caravanserai. Life is returning to the Süleymaniye as some of the buildings are restored; the Evvel and Sani *medreses*, for example, have been converted into one of

Clockwise from far left: The dome of the Süleymaniye Camii; people walking through the porticoed courtyard to the entrance; the octagonal mausoleum of Süleyman, built after his death in 1566; buttresses supporting the central dome; the şadirvan (fountain for ritual ablutions); Muslims cleansing their feet before entering

Istanbul's most important libraries, while the *imaret* (soup kitchen) is now a restaurant.

Interior The prayer hall is a perfect square, and the diameter of the dome is exactly half its height. The other elements in the composition—semi-domes and cupolas, window-lit tympana, galleries and pillars—dance in attendance around this feature. There is little sculptural decoration, but Sinan has allowed other artists free rein, especially on the mihrab wall with its marbles, calligraphy and magnificent stained-glass windows. We know the identity of some artists. The calligrapher (who apparently went blind in the process) was Ahmet Karahisarı; the windows were designed by Ibrahim Sarhoş ('the Drunkard'); the woodwork, inlaid with ivory and mother-of-pearl, is by Ustad Ahmed.

THE BASICS

- D8
- Süleymaniye Caddesi, Süleymaniye
- Daily 9–7
- Beyazıt
- None
- Free/donation

TIP

- Have lunch at Darüzziyafe (▷ 62), the former soup kitchen, now a restaurant with an attractive courtyard garden.

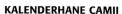

More to See

BOZDOĞAN KEMERI (AQUEDUCT OF VALENS)

This impressive double-arched aqueduct was built in the fourth century AD by Emperor Valens to carry water across the valley between the fourth and the third hills (Fatih to Beyazıt). About 625m (681 yards) of the 1km (0.5 miles) remain and can be seen to best advantage from the grounds of the Şehzade Camii.

B8 Atatürk Bulvari

GALATA KÖPRÜSÜ

Spanning the mouth of the Golden Horn, Galata Bridge is a city landmark. Fishermen dangle their rods from the bridge, ferries bustle to and fro, and restaurants on the lower terraces offer waterfront dining and romantic sunset views. The bridge was built in 1992 after an earlier, much-loved iron bridge was destroyed by fire. The original bridge was rebuilt upstream between Balat and Hasköy and is now called Eski Galata Köprüsü (Old Galata Bridge).

F7 Eminönü, Karaköy

KALENDERHANE CAMII

The 12th-century Byzantine Church of Theotokos Kiriotissa (Our Lady Mother of God) has been painstakingly restored by archaeologists. Inside the caretaker will point out the surviving marble decoration and mosaic fragments from the medieval church, including one of Theotokos Kiriotissa herself and reputedly the earliest fresco depiction of St. Francis of Assisi.

C9 16 Mart Şehitleri Caddesi, Eminönü Daily 9–7 None Free

MIMAR SINAN TÜRBESI

There can be no more fitting memorial to the 16th-century architect of Süleymaniye Camii, Mimar Sinan (▷ 54), than this modest mausoleum, designed by Sinan himself and standing outside the mosque in what used to be the garden of his home.

D8 Mimar Sinan Caddesi, Süleymaniye Mon–Sat 8.30–5 Free

Cars and passers-by are dwarfed by the arches of the Aqueduct of Valens

Dusk on Galata Bridge

NURUOSMANIYE CAMII

Casting a shadow across the Nuruosmaniye Gate of the Covered Bazaar is the mosque that gives it its name, possibly the finest piece of Ottoman baroque architecture in Istanbul. It was completed in 1755 in the reign of Osman III.

E10 Nuruosmaniye Caddesi, Çemberlitaş Daily 9–7 Çemberlitaş None Free

ŞEHZADE CAMII

The 'Prince's Mosque' was built in the 1540s to commemorate Mehmet, son of Süleyman the Magnificent, who died of smallpox aged 21. It was the architect Mimar Sinan's first major commission and has an austere simplicity missing from his later works. The tiling in Mehmet's mausoleum at the side of the mosque is particularly beautiful, creating a paradise garden in green, blue and yellow.

C9 Şehzadebaşı Caddesi, Şehzadebaşı Daily 9–7 None Free

VAKIF HAT SANATLARI MÜZESI (CALLIGRAPHY MUSEUM)

Currently closed for renovation, with plans to reopen in 2016, this is the only museum in the world devoted to the art form of calligraphy. The displays include a reconstruction of a calligraphy workshop.

D10 Beyazıt Meydanı, Beyazıt 212-527-5851 Tue–Sat 9–4 Cafés (€) nearby Beyazıt None Inexpensive

YENI CAMII

This imposing mosque dominates the approaches to Galata Bridge (▷ 56). It was commissioned towards the end of the 16th century, although it was not completed until 1663. The two-story building on the forecourt is the sultan's 'private pew', actually a suite of luxuriously appointed rooms complete with sea views and a private toilet.

F8 Yeni Camii Meydanı, Eminönü Daily 9–7 Cafés (€) nearby Eminönü None Free

The domes of the Şehzade Mosque

A market outside the Yeni Mosque

Two Bazaars

Explore the busy shopping streets of the Tahtakale district on a walk from the Spice Bazaar to the Grand Bazaar.

DISTANCE: 1.5km (1 mile) **ALLOW:** 1 hour

START

EMINÖNÜ
F8 Eminönü

END

KAPALI ÇARŞI
E10 Beyazıt

❶ Begin by the Bosphorus ferry dock at Eminönü, beside the Galata Bridge. Walk through the underpass to arrive outside Yeni Camii (▷ 57).

❷ Keep to the right of the mosque to enter the Spice Bazaar (▷ 52) through the main gate. Enjoy the array of fruits, nuts and spices, then follow the L-shaped bazaar around to the left.

❸ Leave the Spice Bazaar via the Çiçek Pazarı gate, halfway along on the right.

❹ Turn left into Çiçek Pazarı Sokağı, then right into Saka Mehmet Sokağı, which leads into Hacı Küçük Sokağı. Follow this road as it bends to the right.

❺ Turn left into Mahmutpaşa Yokuşu. This hilly street is always swarming with people shopping for cheap clothes and fabrics. After a while you will see the 15th-century Mahmutpaşa baths on your right, now converted into shops.

❻ Climb to the top of Mahmutpaşa Yokuşu to enter the Grand Bazaar (▷ 50–51) through the Mahmutpaşa gate.

❼ Turn left immediately and follow this street around the edge of the bazaar to exit through the Kılıççılar gate. Ahead of you, at the far end of Kılıççılar Sokağı, you can see the Mahmutpaşa Mosque, dating back to the time of Mehmet the Conqueror.

❽ Turn right along the Çarşıkapı Nuruosmaniye Sokağı to end your walk by the Nuruosmaniye gate, one of the many entrances to the Grand Bazaar.

Shopping

ABDULLA

www.abdulla.com

You'll find everything you need for a relaxing Turkish bath—silk and cotton *peştemals* (bath wraps), towels, and olive oil soap—in this small shop right at the heart of the Grand Bazaar.

E10 Halıcılar Caddesi 62, Kapalı Çarşı 212-525-3070 Beyazıt

ADNAN & HASAN

www.adnanandhasan.com

Established in 1978, this shop sells carpets and kilims, as well as tribal and nomadic pieces such as grain sacks and camel saddle-bags.

E10 Halıcılar Caddesi 89, Kapalı Çarşı 212-527-9887 Beyazıt

ALI MUHIDDIN HACI BEKIR

The original Turkish delight shop is still going strong, even after more than 200 years, and is a perennial favorite stop for tourists. It sells a wide variety of gift boxes in tastes ranging from rose-water to lemon, hazelnut and pistachio.

F8 Hamidiye Caddesi 83, Eminönü 212-522-0666 Eminönü

CS IZNIK NICEA CERAMICS

Even in the Grand Bazaar it's hard to miss the shop front of this store with its dazzling display of hand-painted plates and Iznik tiles, of the kind which were used to decorate Istanbul's elaborate mosques.

E10 Takkeciler Caddesi 34–36, Kapalı Çarşı 212-512-2872 Beyazıt

DERVIŞ

www.dervis.com

Similar to Abdulla (▷ this page), Derviş sells eco-friendly bath accessories, organic cotton dressing gowns and natural cosmetics from two shops in the Grand Bazaar. Prices are fixed so there is no need to haggle.

E10 Keseciler Caddesi 33 and Halıcılar Caddesi 51, Kapalı Çarşı 212-514-4525 Beyazıt

ETHNICON

www.ethnicon.com

Ethnicon symbolizes the changing face of the Grand Bazaar, selling a huge range of contemporary kilims and rugs for the modern home, at fixed prices.

E10 Takkeciler Sokağı 58–60, Kapalı Çarşı 212-527-6841 Beyazıt

TURKISH DELIGHT

A box of Turkish delight from Istanbul is always a popular gift. Invented by Ali Muhiddin in 1777 and still sold from the original shop, this sticky treat quickly became popular at the Ottoman court. Known in Turkish as *lokum* (morsel), it is sold all over the city in many shades, shapes and tastes, though the most common is probably the pink variety, which is scented with rosewater.

KAPALI ÇARŞI (GRAND BAZAAR)

See pages 50–51.

KOÇ DERI

www.kocderi.com

There are dozens of outlets in the Grand Bazaar specializing in leather goods, but this is one of the best, with a wide selection of leather jackets and bags. There are several other leather shops on the same street.

E10 Kürkçüler Çarşısı, Kapalı Çarşı 212-527-5553 Beyazıt

KURAKAHVECI MEHMET EFENDI

Just outside the Tahmis entrance to the Spice Bazaar, this is the place to come for Turkish coffee, which arrives with helpful instructions on how to make it. You can also pick up coffee cups and a *cezve*, a long-handled brass pot for making coffee.

E8 Tahmis Sokağı 66, Eminönü 212-511-4262 Eminönü

MALATYA PAZARI

www.mehmetefendi.com

The biggest shop in the Spice Bazaar, you'll want to stop here because it specializes in sun-dried apricots from Malatya, in

eastern Turkey, as well as pistachios, cranberries, stuffed figs and a wide range of other delicious and healthy treats.
F8 Mısır Çarşısı 40–44 212-520-0440 Eminönü

MISIR ÇARŞISI
See page 52.

PUNTO
One attraction here is the setting, in a 17th-century caravanserai, or trading inn, close to the Grand Bazaar; the other is the selection of old and new carpets from all over Turkey.
F10 Gazi Sinanpaşa Sokağı 17 212-511-0853 Çemberlitaş

SAHAFLAR ÇARŞISI
This pretty little lane behind the Beyazıt Mosque has been home to booksellers since Ottoman times, and now houses a daily market of second-hand and antiquarian books, as well as calligraphy and attractively framed Koranic verses.
D10 Sahaflar Çarşısı Sokağı, Beyazıt Beyazıt

ŞENGÖR
This is one of the oldest and most respected carpet dealers in Istanbul, founded in 1918, and now cared for by the fifth generation of the same family. From two shops in the Grand Bazaar it sells beautiful carpets and *kilims* from Turkey and Central Asia.
E10 Takkeciler Sokağı 65, Kapalı Çarşı 212-527-2192 Çemberlitaş

SILK AND CASHMERE
www.silkcashmere.com
Boasting fabrics from Mongolia and China, this is a fine store if you want to stock up on quality cashmere blend cardigans, shawls and sweaters—which are perfect for those chilly winter months.
E10 Kalpakcilar Başi 69 212-526-1251 Beyazıt

ŞIŞKO OSMAN
www.siskoosman.com
This fourth-generation family business has one of the largest selections of handmade carpets and kilims from all over Turkey, and can also design and ship rugs to order for overseas customers. Many of its carpets are original dowry pieces created by Anatolian village women as part of their trousseau, and almost all use natural dyes. The main shop takes up most of Zincirli Han, a historic caravan-serai around a pretty courtyard in the Grand Bazaar.
E10 Zincirli Han 15, Kapalı Çarşı 212-528-3548 Beyazıt

OPENING HOURS
Like most shops in Istanbul, the Grand Bazaar and Spice Bazaar are closed on Sunday. The usual shopping hours are Monday to Saturday 9am– 7pm, though many of the other stores in Sultanahmet stay open late in the evening and on Sunday in summer.

SOFA
www.kashifsofa.com
This Aladdin's Cave near the Grand Bazaar is packed with old maps and prints, silverware, Kütahya pottery and other antiques.
F10 Nuruosmaniye Caddesi 85 212-360-0990 Çemberlitaş

LA TIENDA
Founded in 1923, this gift shop draws inspiration from the city's Jewish and Middle Eastern traditions, with an excellent range of hand-crafted chess and backgammon boards, caskets, silver religious objects, painted miniatures and other souvenirs.
E10 Yağlıkçılar Caddesi 99, Kapalı Çarşı 212-527-5548 Beyazıt

VEFA
This store is famous for the sale of *boza*, a refreshing, vitamin-rich fermented drink, which is said to assist digestion. Taste it before buying a jar to take home.
C8 Katip Celebi Caddesi 104/1 212-519-4922

Entertainment and Nightlife

ÇEMBERLITAŞ HAMAMI
See page 49.

ERENLER
Follow a sign to find the 'Mystic Waterpipe Garden', which is entered via a pretty *medrese* courtyard, with carpet shops down one side and a tea garden on the other. It's popular with both tourists and students from Istanbul.
E10 Yeniçeriler Caddesi 36, Beyazıt 212-528-3785 Daily 7am–midnight Beyazıt

ORIENT HOUSE
www.orienthouseistanbul.com
Located next to the Grand Bazaar, this place offers extravagant dinner shows in an old Ottoman hall, with belly-dancing, folk and wedding dances, whirling dervishes and a military-style Janissary band, accompanied by a four-course meal with beer or wine included.
Off map at E11 Tiyatro Caddesi 25A 212-517-3488 Daily 9pm–midnight Beyazıt

SÜLEYMANIYE HAMAMI
www.suleymaniyehamami.com
Unusually, these baths are mixed-sex, which means men and women bathe together, though all the masseurs are male. This makes the baths a good choice for couples, but single women may feel uncomfortable here. Transfer from your hotel is included in the price.
D8 Mimar Sinan Caddesi 20, Süleymaniye 212-520-3410 Daily 7am–midnight

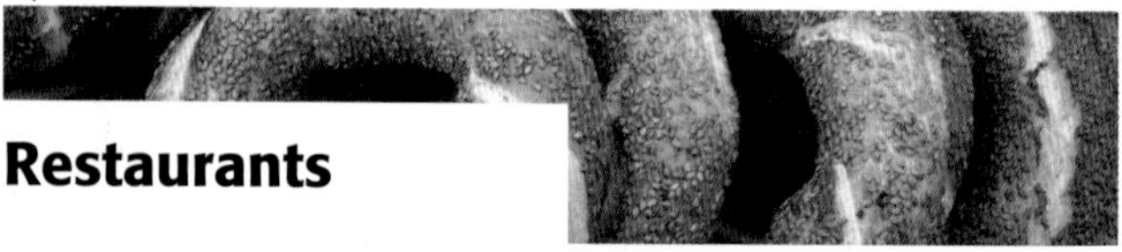

Restaurants

PRICES

Prices are approximate, based on a three-course meal for one person.

€€€	over 50 TL
€	30–50 TL
€	under 30 TL

DARÜZZIYAFE (€€)
www.daruzziyafe.com.tr
Traditional Turkish cuisine in the Süleymaniye Mosque *imaret* (soup kitchen), and courtyard garden. No alcohol.
D8 Şifahane Sokağı 6, Süleymaniye 212-511-8415 Daily 12–11

HAMDI ET LOKANTASI (€€)
A cake shop masks the entrance to this restaurant, serving kebabs, grilled meat and Turkish dishes, on a rooftop terrace with views of Galata Bridge and the Golden Horn.
E8 Kalçin Sokağı 17, Eminönü 212-528-0390 Daily 12–11

BALIK EKMEK

The quintessential Istanbul street food is *balık ekmek* (fish in bread), a grilled mackerel sandwich which was traditionally sold to hungry customers straight from the fishing boats beside Galata Bridge. These days, however, the sandwich is mainly sold from stalls on the quayside, but the aroma of grilled fish still hangs over Eminönü each evening. A portion of *balık ekmek* with salad makes an inexpensive, filling and deliciously healthy snack. Sprinkle with a little salt and lemon juice, then sit down on a bench to enjoy the view.

PANDELI (€€)
www.pandeli.com
Housed in the former guardhouse of the Spice Bazaar and decorated with blue ceramic tiles, this famous restaurant specializes in aubergine (eggplant) *börek* and sea bass *en papillotte*.
F8 Mısır Çarşısı 1, Eminönü 212-527-3909 Mon–Sat 12–4 Eminönü

Western Districts

The traditional religious districts of Fener, Balat and Eyüp lie on the south bank of the Haliç (Golden Horn). They form a fascinating area of churches, mosques and historic Greek and Jewish districts within the city walls.

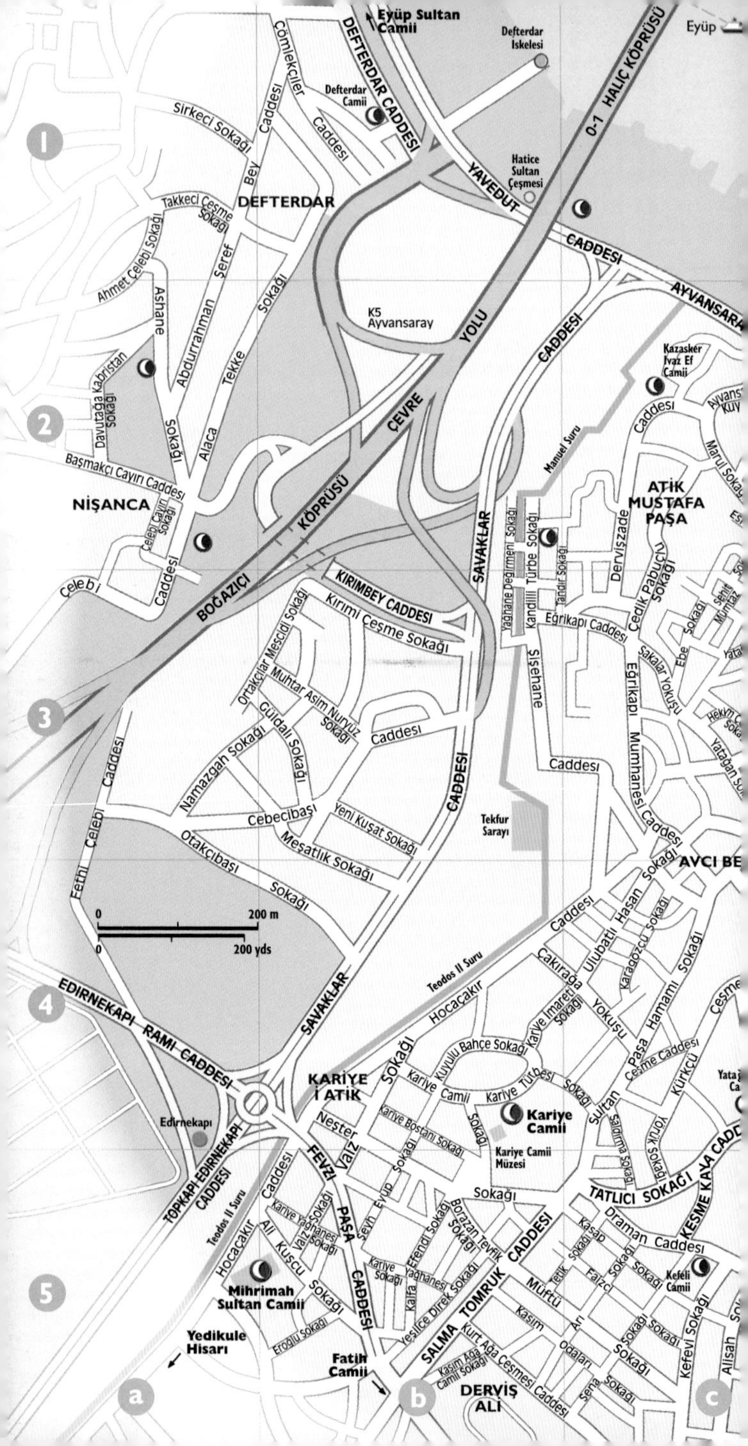
Eyüp Sultan Camii
Eyüp
Defterdar Iskelesi
Defterdar Camii
DEFTERDAR CADDESI
O-1 HALIÇ KÖPRÜSÜ
Çömlekçiler Caddesi
Sirkeci Sokağı
Bey Caddesi
Hatice Sultan Çeşmesi
YAVEDUT CADDESI
AYVANSARAY
DEFTERDAR
Takkeci Çeşme Sokağı
Ahmet Çelebi Sokağı
Ashane
Şeref Sokağı
Abdurrahman
Tekke
K5 Ayvansaray
YOLU
ÇEVRE
CADDESI
Kazasker Ivaz Ef Camii
Davutağa Kabristan Sokağı
Alaca
Sokağı
Caddesi
Manuel Suru
Başmakçı Çayırı Caddesi
ATİK MUSTAFA PAŞA
NİŞANCA
Çelebi Çayırı Sokağı
KÖPRÜSÜ
SAVAKLAR
Yağhane Değirmeni Sokağı
Kandilli Türbe Sokağı
Tandır Sokağı
Dervişzade
Çedik Pabuçlu Sokağı
Çelebi
Caddesi
BOĞAZIÇI
KIRIMBEY CADDESI
Kırımi Çeşme Sokağı
Eğrikapı Caddesi
Ortakçılar Mescidi Sokağı
Muhtar Asim Nuryüz Sokağı
Şişehane
Sakalar Yokuşu
Ebe
Eğrikapı Mumhanesi Caddesi
Güldalı Sokağı
Caddesi
Namazgah Sokağı
Caddesi
Cebecibaşı
Yeni Kuşat Sokağı
Mesatlik Sokağı
Otakçıbaşı Sokağı
Fethi Çelebi Caddesi
Tekfur Sarayı
AVCI BE
0
200 m
0
200 yds
Teodos II Suru
Hocaçakır
Çakırağa
Ulubatlı Hasan Sokağı
Karagözcü Sokağı
Hamamı Sokağı
EDIRNEKAPI RAMI CADDESI
SAVAKLAR
Kariye İmareti Sokağı
Yokuşu
Kuyulu Bahçe Sokağı
Paşa
Çeşme Caddesi
KARİYE İ ATİK
Kariye Camii
Kariye Türbesi
Sokağı
Kürkçü
Neşter
Kariye Bostanı Sokağı
Kariye Camii
Sultan
Edirnekapı
Kariye Camii Müzesi
Sadırma Sokağı
Yörük Sokağı
TOPKAPI EDIRNEKAPI CADDESI
FEVZI PAŞA CADDESI
Vaiz
Sokağı
Sokağı
TATLICI SOKAĞI
KESME KAYA CADD
Teodos II Suru
Caddesi
Kariye Yağhanesi Sokağı
Ali Kuşçu
Şeyh Eyüp
Efendi Sokağı
Borazan Tevfik Sokağı
SALMA TOMRUK CADDESI
Draman Caddesi
Kasap
Tetik Sokağı
Faizci
Sokağı
Kefeli Camii
Hocaçakır
Mihrimah Sultan Camii
Kariye Sokağı
Yağhanesi
Kalfa
Yesilce Direk Sokağı
Müftü
Kasım
Arı
Odaları
Sokağı
Kefevi Sokağı
Alişah
Yedikule Hisarı
Eroğlu Sokağı
Fatih Camii
Kurt Ağa Çeşmesi Caddesi
Kasım Ağa Camii Sokağı
Sena Sokağı
DERVİŞ ALİ
1
2
3
4
5
a
b
c

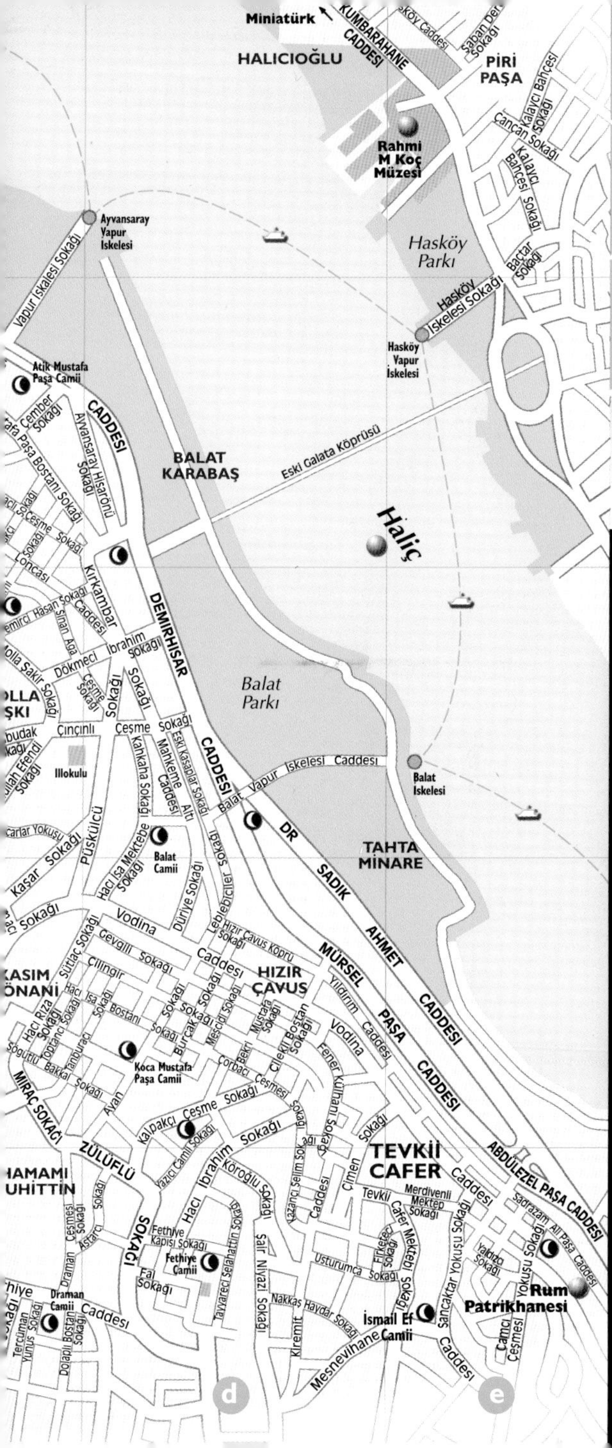
Miniatürk
KUMBARAHANE CADDESİ
HALICIOĞLU
PİRİ PAŞA
Kalaycı Bahçesi Sokağı
Çançan Sokağı
Rahmi M Koç Müzesi
Ayvansaray Vapur İskelesi
Hasköy Parkı
Vapur İskelesi Sokağı
Baçtar Sokağı
Hasköy İskelesi Sokağı
Hasköy Vapur İskelesi
Atik Mustafa Paşa Camii
Ayvansaray Hisarönü Sokağı
CADDESİ
Eski Galata Köprüsü
BALAT KARABAŞ
Haliç
Kırkambar Sokağı
Sinan Ağa Caddesi
DEMİRHİSAR CADDESİ
Dökmeci İbrahim Sokağı
Balat Parkı
Çınçınlı Çeşme Sokağı
İllokulu
Kahkaha Sokağı
Mankeme Caddesi
Eski Kasaplar Sokağı
Balat Vapur İskelesi Caddesi
Balat İskelesi
Püskülcü
Hacı İsa Mektebe Sokağı
Balat Camii
DR SADIK AHMET CADDESİ
TAHTA MİNARE
Kasar Sokağı
Vodina Caddesi
Dürüye Sokağı
Leblebiciler Sokağı
Hızır Çavuş Köprü Sokağı
Gevgili Sokağı
Çilingir
HIZIR ÇAVUŞ
MÜRSEL PAŞA CADDESİ
Yıldırım Caddesi
Koca Mustafa Paşa Camii
Fener Külhanı Sokağı
MİRAÇ SOKAĞI
ZÜLÜFLÜ SOKAĞI
Kalpakçı Çeşme Sokağı
Yazıcı Camii Sokağı
Hacı İbrahim Sokağı
Köroğlu Sokağı
TEVKİİ CAFER
ABDÜLEZEL PAŞA CADDESİ
Sadrazam Ali Paşa Caddesi
Fethiye Kapısı Sokağı
Fethiye Camii
Şair Nİyazi Sokağı
Usturumca Sokağı
Sancaktar Yokuşu Sokağı
Rum Patrikhanesi
Draman Camii
Draman Caddesi
Nakkaş Haydar Sokağı
İsmail Ef Camii
Mesnevihane Caddesi
Kiremit
d
e

Eyüp Sultan Camii

TOP 25

HIGHLIGHTS

- Wishing window
- Prophet's footprint

TIP

- Take the cable car behind the mosque to reach the Pierre Loti Café (www.atalatur.com), named after a 19th-century French writer and naval officer who lived in Istanbul and loved the views over the Golden Horn from this spot.

Eyüp is one of the holiest sites in Islam. Crowds of pilgrims descend here on Fridays and religious holidays to make their devotions. The market stalls along the route to the mosque do a brisk trade in religious paraphernalia.

Shrine Eyüp Ensari, standard-bearer and close companion of the Prophet Muhammad, fell in battle during the Arab siege of Constantinople in AD674–78. His burial place was rediscovered in 1453 by Akşemseddin, tutor of Mehmet the Conqueror, and the delighted sultan erected a shrine on the site.

Mosque and türbe (mausoleum) The original mosque was destroyed during the earthquake of 1766 and rebuilt by Selim III. A fine example

This striking mosque complex includes the mausoleum of Eyüp Ensari, a close friend of the Prophet Muhammad, and is one of the most sacred sites in Islam

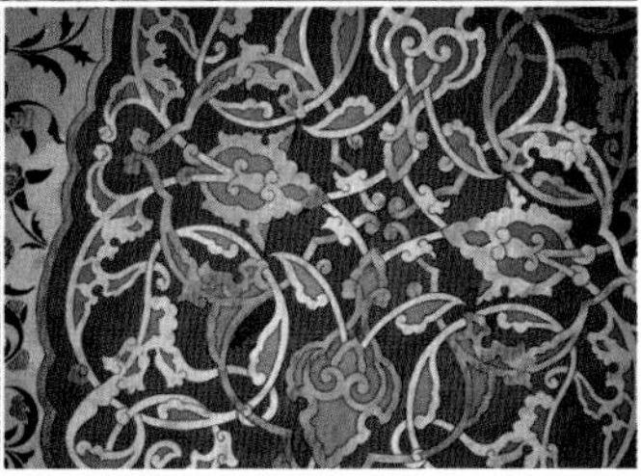

of Ottoman baroque, the interior is highlighted with gold leaf on white marble. Many young boys come here on Sunday morning, dressed in white suits for their circumcision. After praying at the mosque, pious Muslims make their way to the octagonal mausoleum of Eyüp Ensari. Dating from 1485, the *türbe* is decorated with blue, white and henna-red tiles from Iznik and Kütahya. Worshippers pause at the 'wishing window' (protected by a golden grille) before filing past the sarcophagus. Preserved in one corner is a cast of the Prophet Muhammad's footprint.

Cemetery A stroll through the hillside cemetery, its faded marble tombstones and crooked stelae half-hidden by cypresses, is a perfect way to round off a visit.

THE BASICS

Off map at b1

Camii Kebir Caddesi, Eyüp

Mosque: daily 9–7. Mausoleum of Eyüp: daily 9.30–4.30

Lots of cafés and restaurants (€–€€€); Pierre Loti Café (€; ▷ Tip, 66)

Eyüp Iskelesi

None

Free/donation

No photography in Eyüp mausoleum

Kariye Camii

TOP 25

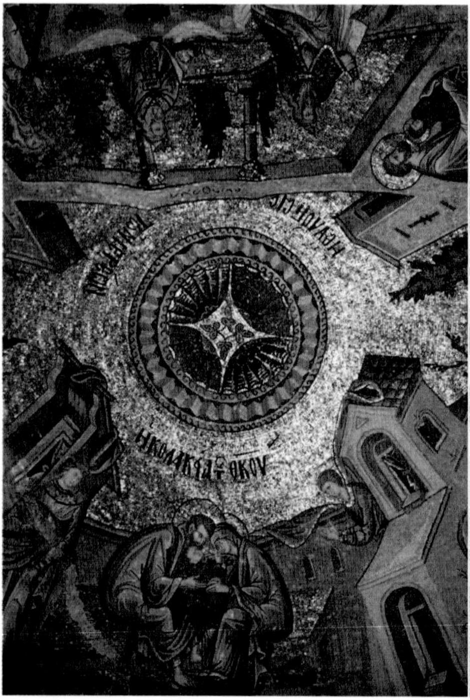

HIGHLIGHTS

- Christ Pantocrator (mosaic)
- Miracle at Cana (mosaic)
- Metochites presenting Chora to Christ (mosaic)
- Last Judgement (fresco)
- Resurrection (fresco)
- Mother of God (fresco)

TIP

- Asitane (▷ 74) in the Kariye Hotel makes a delightful spot for lunch after visiting the church.

The lovely old Church of St. Savior of Chora houses some of the world's most precious Byzantine mosaics and frescos. The dramatic rendering of the Resurrection in the apse seems to speak directly to us across seven centuries.

Metochites' church The Church of St. Savior in Chora (now the Kariye Camii Museum) was built between 1316 and 1321, and incorporates the shell of an earlier church. Chora means 'in the country', an allusion to an even older foundation outside the city walls. The church's patron was Metochites, who served the Emperor Andronicus II Palaelogus as prime minister and treasurer. When the emperor was overthrown in 1328, Metochites was sent into exile. Two years later he was allowed

The wonderful mosaics and frescos in the Church of St. Savior in Chora were probably the work of just one artist

to return as a monk to live out his days in the confines of the church he had founded.

Mosaics and frescos Fortunately, the church's glorious mosaics and frescos were not destroyed when the building was converted into a mosque in 1511. They are almost certainly the work of a single unknown artist, whose signature style is in the hooked tails of the drapery and the peculiar 'shadows' around the feet. The mosaics depict the life and ministry of Christ and also the Virgin Mary. Above the door leading into the nave is Metochites presenting his church to Christ; he is wearing the typical Byzantine sun hat known as a *skiadon*. The frescos are confined to the *parekklesion* and, as befits a mortuary chapel, depict the Last Judgement and the Harrowing of Hell.

THE BASICS

b4

Kariye Camii Sokağı, Edirnekapı

212-631-9241

Thu–Tue 9–5 (summer 9–7)

Cafés (€) on square; Asitane (▷ Tip, 74)

None

Moderate

No flash photography

Yedikule Hisarı

TOP 25

Yedikule Castle (left and right) forms part of the city walls

THE BASICS

- Off map at a5
- Yedikule Meydanı
- 212-585-8933
- Daily 8.30–5
- Cafés (€) nearby
- Yedikule
- 80
- None
- Inexpensive

HIGHLIGHTS

- Well of Blood
- View from the battlements
- Porta Aurea

TIP

- To explore the land walls in greater depth, follow the walk on page 73.

You could spend a whole day exploring the old Byzantine fortifications, with their watchtowers, gateways and parapets. Access is virtually unrestricted and the views are superb.

The land walls Stretching all the way from the Sea of Marmara to the Golden Horn, Constantinople's land walls enclosed the entire Byzantine city. They were built in AD412–22 during the reign of Theodosius II and, apart from severe structural damage sustained during an earthquake in 447, survived almost intact until they were finally breached in 1453 by Sultan Mehmet the Conqueror.

Yedikule Castle The Fortress of the Seven Towers assumed its present form around 1460 when Mehmet added five towers to the Porta Aurea (Golden Gate). Dating from AD390, this was originally a free-standing triumphal arch used exclusively by emperors to enter the city. The gate still exists, although the gold-plated doors and statues have long since disappeared and the arches themselves have been bricked up. First used as a treasury, the castle became a notorious place of imprisonment. In one of the towers is the cell where, in 1622, the deposed sultan, Osman II, was murdered by the traditional method of strangulation by bowstring—while simultaneously having his testicles crushed. You can also see the Well of Blood into which severed heads were unceremoniously tossed.

More to See

FATIH CAMII

Named after the conqueror of Constantinople, Sultan Fatih Mehmet, this important mosque complex actually dates from 1767. Its predecessor (built in 1463–70) was completely destroyed by an earthquake. You can see Mehmet's tomb in front of the mihrab wall.

Off map at b5 · Fevzi Paşa Caddesi, Fatih · Daily 9–7 · Cafés (€), restaurants (€€) nearby · None · Free

HALIÇ (GOLDEN HORN)

An inlet of the Bosphorus around 8km (5 miles) in length, the Golden Horn has long provided a natural port for Istanbul. Ferries leave hourly from a pier behind Eminönü bus station, to the left of Galata Bridge. The boats criss-cross between the northern and southern shores, stopping at Kasimpaşa, Fener, Hasköy, Ayvansaray and Sütlüce on their way to Eyüp (▷ 66–67).

d2 · Eminönü

MIHRIMAH SULTAN CAMII

The patron of this beautiful mosque, Mihrimah Sultan, was the favorite daughter of Süleyman the Magnificent and the richest woman in the world at the time. She shared a passion for architecture with her husband, Rüstem Paşa, and they were patrons of Mimar Sinan, the great builder. With the Mihrimah Sultan Mosque, Sinan created a prototype for mosque design that endured throughout the Ottoman era. The focal point is the huge cuboid prayer hall, covered by a dome 36.5m (120ft) high and 20m (66ft) across. The sense of space is achieved by banishing the galleries to domed bays at the north and south ends. With this uninterrupted view, you can appreciate the magnificent decoration as you look up to the arabesque stencils between the supporting arches and across to the tiling of the mihrab wall.

a5 · Ali Kuşçu Sokağı, Edirnekapı · Daily 9–7 · Cafés (€) nearby · Edirnekapı · None · Free

The waters of the Golden Horn

The dome and minarets of Fatih Mosque

MINIATÜRK

www.miniaturk.com.tr

Opened in 2003, this amusement park features a walk past miniature reproductions of more than 100 Turkish buildings, from palaces and mosques to airports, shopping malls and a football stadium.

Off map at d1 Imrahor Caddesi, Sütlüce 212-222-2882 Summer daily 9–8, winter Mon–Fri 9–5, Sat–Sun 9–8 Café (€) and restaurant (€€) 47C, 47E Sütlüce, then short bus or *dolmuş* ride Moderate

RAHMI M. KOÇ MÜZESI

www.rmk-museum.org.tr

Visitors of all ages will enjoy this hands-on transport museum, with vintage trams, cars, boats, planes and even a submarine on display in a converted foundry beside the Golden Horn. It also displays models and toys.

e1 Hasköy Caddesi 27, Hasköy 212-369-6600 Tue–Fri 10–5, Sat–Sun 10–7 Café (€) and restaurants (▷ 74) Sütlüce Good Moderate

RUM PATRIKHANESI (ECUMENICAL ORTHODOX PATRIARCHATE)

www.patriarchate.org

The district of Fener is the traditional home of Istanbul's Greek community and the worldwide home of the Eastern Orthodox church, which continued to be based in Constantinople even after the Ottoman conquest. As the ecumenical patriarch of the Orthodox communion, the Archbishop of Constantinople and New Rome is the spiritual leader of 250 million Christians in Russia, Greece and elsewhere. His seat, the cathedral of St. George, was completed in 1720 as a three-aisled basilica. The Divine Liturgy is held here every Sunday morning and the church is the focus of Orthodox celebrations at Easter.

e5 Sadrazam Ali Paşa Caddesi, Fener 212-531-9670 Daily 9–5 Cafés (€) and restaurants (€€) nearby; (Tarihi Haliç Işkembecisi, ▷ 74) Fener Free/donation

Lighting candles in the Ecumenical Orthodox Patriarchate

Exploring the Walls

Take a walk in the shadow of the fifth-century Byzantine walls, which protected the city for a 1,000 years.

DISTANCE: 2.5km (1.5 miles) **ALLOW:** 1 hour

START

TEKFUR SARAYI

b3 Ayvansaray

END

TOPKAPI

Off map at a5 Topkapı

❶ Start at Tekfur Sarayı, the ruined 13th-century palace on Şişehane Caddesi near the northern end of the walls. The palace is undergoing long-term restoration but still makes an impressive sight.

❷ Walk south along Hocaçakır Caddesi, following a section of newly restored walls. You can climb the steps to the top in places, but take care as there are no rails to prevent you falling.

❸ When you reach a busy road junction, cross Fevzi Paşa Caddesi and take the steps beside the tower on the far side.

❹ Pass the remains of Edirnekapı on your right. It was through this gate that Sultan Mehmet the Conqueror first breached the walls and entered the city in 1453.

❺ Just beyond Edirnekapı, you pass Mihrimah Sultan Camii (▷ 71) on your left.

❻ The walk continues along the inside of the city walls. The next stretch takes you along Sulukule Caddesi, through the somewhat run-down Sulukule district, the traditional home of Istanbul's Roma (gypsy) community.

❼ Take great care crossing the busy Adnan Menderes Caddesi and continue along the walls to Topkapı, the 'Cannon Gate', also breached by Mehmet the Conqueror in 1453. Here you will find buses, trams and taxis to take you back to the city.

❽ For a longer walk, you can continue along the outside of the walls all the way to Yedikule Hisarı (▷ 70).

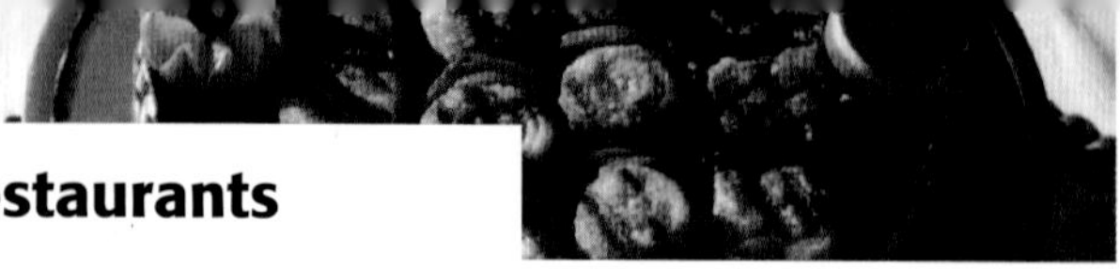

Restaurants

PRICES

Prices are approximate, based on a three-course meal for one person.

€€€	more than 50 TL
€€	30–50 TL
€	under 30 TL

ASITANE (€€€)

www.asitanerestaurant.com

This hotel restaurant beside Kariye Camii re-creates authentic Ottoman recipes, including several dishes served at a circumcision feast in 1539 for Süleyman the Magnificent's sons. How about sampling the almond and coconut soup followed by melon stuffed with mincemeat, rice, almonds, currants and pistachios? In summer you can dine in the pretty garden.

b5 Kariye Camii Sokaşı 18, Edirnekapı 212-635-7997 Daily 11.30am–midnight Edirnekapı

CAFÉ DU LEVANT (€€)

This is one of two restaurants belonging to the Rahmi M. Koç Museum (▷ 72), both of which offer alternatives to the standard repertoire of Turkish cuisine. The aim of Café du Levant is to re-create an authentic Parisian brasserie on the streets of Istanbul. The decor reflects this, with stained glass, tiled floors, wooden tables and French posters on the walls, while the menu features classic French dishes and an excellent range of wines.

e1 Hasköy Caddesi 27, Hasköy 212-369-6607 Tue–Sun 10–10 Hasköy

DEVELI (€€)

Established in 1912, this popular restaurant in Samatya serves the best kebabs in town, including aubergine (eggplant), pistachio, yoghurt and garlic kebabs, as well as an excellent selection of *mezes*, salads and *pide* bread. Ask for a table on the fifth-floor terrace with views over the Sea of Marmara.

Off map at a12 Gümüşyüzük Sokaşı 7 212-529-0833 Daily 12–12 Koca Mustafa Paşa

MEZES

In a typical Istanbul restaurant, you will be offered a selection of hot and cold appetizers known collectively as *mezes*. These dishes are often suitable for vegetarians and range from simple salads dressed in olive oil to aubergine (eggplant) purée and Çengelköy cucumbers, and from *biber dolması* (green peppers stuffed with raisins, rice and pine nuts) to fried *kalamar* with *tarator* (breadcrumbs flavored with garlic and walnut), Albanian diced liver and pastries seasoned with fresh herbs. *Mezes* are usually accompanied by fresh white bread.

KARIYE PEMBE KÖŞK (€)

With tables on a pretty square facing Kariye Camii and a simple menu of toasted sandwiches, kebabs and lentil soup, this makes a good choice for a quick lunch after visiting the museum.

b4 Kariye Camii Sokaşı 27 212-635-8586 Daily 9am–11pm Edirnekapı

TARIHI HALIÇ IŞKEMBECIŞI (€€)

www.haliciskembecisi.com

On the seafront at Fener and just around the corner from the Greek Patriarchate (▷ 72), this traditional Turkish restaurant serves delicious Anatolian soups as well as succulent grilled meat dishes and kebabs. The restaurant still commemorates the death of founding Turkish President, Kemal Atatürk, with a display of photographs in the memorial room upstairs (the restaurant was founded in the same year as his death—1938).

e5 Abdulezelpaşa Caddesi 117, Haliç–Fener 212-534-9419 Daily 24 hours Fener

Beyoğlu

Cross the Galata Bridge from Eminönü and you leave old Istanbul behind. This is Beyoğlu, the 19th-century European quarter north of the Golden Horn, whose central boulevard, Istiklâl Caddesi, buzzes with activity day and night.

Top 25 TOP 25

1
2
3
4
5
6
D
E
F
0
200 m
0
200 yds
TARLABAŞI
Kamer Hatun Camii
KAMER HATUN
HAMALBAŞI
Balık Sokağı
Kalyoncu Caddesi
Meşrutiyet Caddesi
Hacıpulo Sokağı
Tepebaşı Parkı
REFİK SAĞLAM CADDESİ
Ist Sergi Sarayı Odakule
Kallavi Sokağı
Eski Çiçek
Nuru Ziya
Pera Palas Oteli
Pera Müzesi
İstiklâl Caddesi
Balyoz Sokağı
Piremeci Sokağı
Saint Antoine Kilisesi
Tomtom
EVLİYA ÇELEBİ
Kuytu Sokağı
Asmalı Mescit Sokağı
Gönül Sokağı
Minare Sokağı
Şehbender Sokağı
Jurnal Sokağı
Simal Sokağı
ASMALI MESCİT
Sofyalı Sokağı
Müeyyet Sokağı
Ayhan Işık Sokağı
Sümbül Sokağı
Tünel Geçidi
Kumbaracı
Tercüman
Bedrettin Sokağı
Nergis Sokağı
Müellif
Şahkulu Bostanı Sokağı
Edebiyat
Şişhane
Tünel
Tünel Caddesi
OKÇU MUSA CADDESİ
Caddesi
Belediye Caddesi
Galata Mevlevihanesi
ŞAHKULU
İskender
Şişhane Sokağı
Büyük Hendek
Yolcuzade
Neve Shalom Sinagog
Tünel
Dede
Serdar-ı Ekrem
Ali Hoca
Dibek Sokağı
Mektebe Sokağı
Tutsak Sokağı
Küçük Hendek Sokağı
Şahkulu Sokağı
Timarcı Sokağı
Galip
Harup Sokağı
Emek Yemez Sokağı
Dik Sokağı
Okçumusa Camii
Simsir Sokağı
Galata Kulesi
Tatar Beyi Sokağı
Ali Hoca Aralığı
Hoca Camii
Mürver Sokağı
Laleli Çeşme Sokağı
Yüksek Kaldırım Caddesi
Lüleci Hendek
Azapkapı Çeşmesi
Yolcuzade Sokağı
Yanıkkapı Sokağı
Ziya Paşa Caddesi
BEREKETZADE
MÜEYYET
Galata Kulesi Sokağı
Camekan Sokağı
ATATÜRK KÖPRÜSÜ
Azapkapı Sokullu M Paşa Camii
EMEK YEMEZ
TERSANE CADDESİ
Buğulu Sokağı
Abdül Selah Sokağı
Arap Camii
Ala Geyik Sokağı
Kart Çınar Sokağı
Hacı Ali Sokağı
KEMERALTI
Hoca Hanım Sokağı
Hediye Sokağı
Eski Tayyare Çıkmazı
Galata Mahkemesi Sokağı
Perşembe Pazarı Caddesi
BANKALAR CADDESİ
Banker Sokağı
Türk Musevileri Müzesi
Yemeneciler Caddesi
Kalafatçılar Caddesi
Bakır Sokağı
Samur Sokağı
Zincirli Han Sokağı
Bereketzade Sokağı
Söğüt Sokağı
Perçemli Sokağı
HARACI ALİ SOKAĞI
KARAKÖY CADDESİ
Necatibey
Yeraltı Camii
Karaköy
SEBAHATTİN EVREN CADDESİ
Mumhane Caddesi
Haliç
Makaracılar Caddesi
Fermeneciler Caddesi
Karaköy
Kemankeş Caddesi
ARAP CAMİİ
RIHTIM CADDESİ
Haliç
GALATA KÖPRÜSÜ
Karaköy Vapur İskelesi

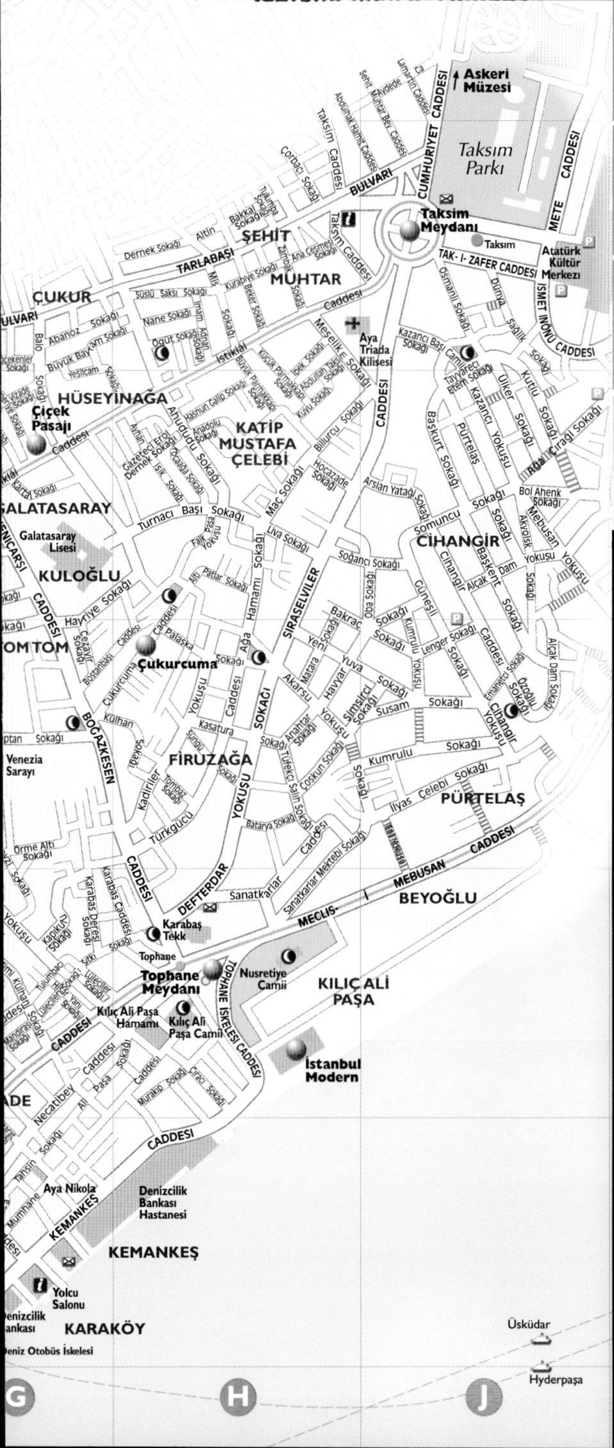
Askeri Müzesi
Taksim Parkı
CUMHURIYET CADDESI
METE CADDESI
Taksim Meydanı
Taksim
TAK- I- ZAFER CADDESI
Atatürk Kültür Merkezi
ISMET INÖNÜ CADDESI
Taksim Caddesi
Çorbacı Sokağı
BULVARI
ŞEHİT MUHTAR
TARLABAŞI
Dernek Sokağı
ÇUKUR
HÜSEYİNAĞA
Çiçek Pasajı
İstiklal Caddesi
Aya Triada Kilisesi
KATİP MUSTAFA ÇELEBİ
GALATASARAY
Galatasaray Lisesi
KULOĞLU
TOMTOM
Çukurcuma
FİRUZAĞA
CİHANGİR
SIRASELVILER
Turnacı Başı Sokağı
Soğancı Sokağı
Venezia Sarayı
BOĞAZKESEN
DEFTERDAR
Karabaş Tekk
Tophane
Tophane Meydanı
TOPHANE İSKELESİ CADDESİ
Nusretiye Camii
KILIÇ ALİ PAŞA
Kılıç Ali Paşa Hamamı
Kılıç Ali Paşa Camii
İstanbul Modern
MECLIS- I- MEBUSAN CADDESI
BEYOĞLU
PÜRTELAŞ
Denizcilik Bankası Hastanesi
Aya Nikola
KEMANKEŞ
Yolcu Salonu
KARAKÖY
Deniz Otobüs İskelesi
Üsküdar
Hyderpaşa
G
H
J

Istanbul Modern

TOP 25

HIGHLIGHTS

- *Han Coffee House* by Bedri Rahmi Eyüboğlu
- *Music Shop at Tünel* by Muhçin Kut
- *Kapı (Door)* by Burhan Uygur
- *Stairway to Hell* by Monica Bonvicini

TIP

- Visit the museum on a Thursday, when there is free admission and extended opening hours.

With contemporary Turkish and international art housed in a dramatic waterfront setting, this modern art museum aims to put Istanbul on the European cultural map, alongside London, Paris and Barcelona.

The building Istanbul Modern opened in December 2004 in a former customs warehouse on the pier at Karaköy. The lower floor is given over to temporary exhibitions and a photography gallery, cinema and new media room, while the permanent exhibition is upstairs in the main hall. With its sleek white walls and picture windows giving views across the Bosphorus to Topkapı Palace, it makes a stunning setting for a display of 20th-century Turkish art.

Istanbul Modern, in a former customs warehouse, displays contemporary art

The collection The items in the permanent collection are rotated annually but are mostly arranged by themes such as landscapes, city life, self-portraits and abstract art. In addition, there are entire galleries dedicated to individual Turkish painters, including Ihsan Cemal Karaburçak (1897–1970), an abstract artist who took up painting only at the age of 33. You cannot miss *Stairway to Hell*, by Venetian artist Monica Bonvicini, a tortured structure of steel chains and broken glass that stands at the heart of the main hall, acting both as a piece of installation art and as the staircase between the upper and lower galleries.

Light relief When you need a break, the museum café has a delightful terrace beside the Bosphorus.

THE BASICS

www.istanbulmodern.org
H5
Meclis-i Mebusan Caddesi, Karaköy
212-334-7300
Tue, Wed, Fri–Sun 10–6, Thu 10–8
Café and restaurant (€€)
Tophane
Fully accessible
Moderate (free on Thu)
Free guided tours at 3 and 5 Thu and Sun. Audio guides inexpensive

Istiklâl Caddesi

TOP 25

HIGHLIGHTS

- Tünel funicular and tram
- Galatasaray Lycée
- Church of St. Mary Draperis
- Church of St. Anthony of Padua
- Çiçek Pasajı (▷ 82)

TIP

- Take the old-fashioned funicular from Karaköy to Tünel, walk along Istiklâl Caddesi, then take the modern funicular from Taksim to Kabataş to return to Karaköy by tram.

Independence Avenue is Istanbul's most popular promenade and the focus of evening entertainment. A nostalgic tram journey takes you the entire length of the pedestrianized shopping street, from Tünel to Taksim Square.

Grande Rue de Pera In the 19th century, this was the Grande Rue de Pera, the central thoroughfare of Istanbul's European quarter. Most of the foreign embassies were located here, along with churches, grand apartment blocks and fashionable hotels. Visitors arriving on the Orient Express and taking the funicular to Tünel christened Istanbul 'the Paris of the East'. But after the Turkish capital moved to Ankara in 1923, the ambassadors relocated and Pera went into decline.

Istiklâl Caddesi is the place to be seen in Istanbul

A street for strolling Today, Istiklâl Caddesi has recovered its former cachet and is once again the place to be seen in Istanbul. Music blares out of cafés day and night, and the street is lined with bookstores, cinemas, art galleries and clothes shops. Pedestrianization has given the area a new lease of life; on weekend afternoons, half of Istanbul seems to be strolling here and showing off the latest fashions.

Vintage tram If you don't want to walk, take the antique tram that rattles up and down between Tünel and Taksim Square, pausing halfway outside the 19th-century Galatasaray Lycée. The trams stopped service in 1961 but were reintroduced 30 years later during a wave of nostalgia.

THE BASICS

- G4
- Lots of cafés (€) and restaurants (€€) in nearby streets
- Funicular to Tünel or Taksim
- Taksim

More to See

ASKERI MÜZESI

Walk up Cumhuriyet Caddesi from Taksim Square to reach the Military Museum, with its vast collection of Ottoman and Turkish weapons, uniforms and flags. Dedicated to one thousand years of military history it is well worth a visit. Arrive before 3pm for the daily concert of clashing cymbals, pipes and drums by the Mehter military orchestra, a marching band resplendent in red Ottoman uniforms.

Off map at J1 Vali Konaği Caddesi, Harbiye 212-233-2720 Wed–Sun 9–5 Osmanbey Inexpensive

ÇIÇEK PASAJI

A 19th-century shopping arcade off Istiklâl Caddesi (▷ 80–81), the elegant Çiçek Pasajı (Flower Passage) houses several *meyhanes* (▷ panel, 88) where musicians perform most nights. The adjoining street, Sahne Sokağı, is the Balık Pazarı (Fish Market).

G3 Taksim; funicular to Tünel Taksim

ÇUKURCUMA

The steeply sloping streets behind Galatasaray Lycée lead to this attractive residential district, home to Istanbul's largest concentration of antiques shops. The best places for browsing are along Faik Paşa Yokuşu and Çukurcuma Caddesi. For upscale dining options, explore the cafés, bistros and patisseries of Cezayir Caddesi, also known as La Rue Française. This street of 19th-century houses was restored in 2004 with the assistance of the municipality of Paris, which provided the gas lamps.

G4–H4 Taksim; funicular to Tünel

GALATA KULESI

www.galatatower.net

A steep climb up Galata Kulesi Sokağı or a short walk downhill from Tünel leads to the round Galata Tower, built as a Genoese fortification in 1348 and later used as a barracks, prison and astronomical observatory. Take the lift to the viewing platform for sunset

A night scene in Çiçek Pasajı

views. At night, the tower is used for belly-dancing shows (▷ 87).
F5 · Galata Meydanı, Tünel · 212-293-8180 · Daily 9–8 · Funicular to Tünel · Moderate

GALATA MEVLEVIHANESI

This *tekke* (dervish lodge) was closed in the 1920s but is now the Museum of Classical Literature. The tomb of 17th-century Sufi poet Galip Dede stands in the garden. The main reason to come here is to see the mystical whirling dervish ceremony (▷ 86; panel, 87).
F5 · Galip Dede Caddesi 15, Tünel · 212-245-4141 · Wed–Mon 9.30–4.30 · Funicular to Tünel · Inexpensive

PERA MÜZESI

www.peramuzesi.org.tr

This excellent private museum opened in 2005 in the former Hotel Bristol, built in 1893 during the grand old days of Pera. The permanent exhibition, displayed over two floors, features an eclectic collection of Anatolian weights and measures, Kütahya ceramics and Ottoman-era portraits by European Orientalist painters. Look for *The Tortoise Trainer*, the best-known work by Turkish archaeologist and artist Osman Hamdi Bey (1842–1910).
G4 · Meşrutiyet Caddesi 65, Tepebaşı · 212-334-9900 · Tue–Sat 10–7, Sun 12–6 · Café (€) · Good · Funicular to Tünel · Inexpensive

PERA PALAS OTELI

www.perapalace.com

The grande dame of Istanbul hotels opened in 1892 for passengers arriving on the Orient Express. Among the guests was crime writer Agatha Christie, who stayed in Room 411 while writing *Murder on the Orient Express*. The hotel reopened in September 2010 after extensive renovation. Staff will take visitors up in the birdcage lift (the oldest electric elevator in Istanbul) to see Christie's room—when it is not being used by guests—and the Museum Room

You can see whirling dervishes at Galata Mevlevihanesi

The Galata Tower, from across the Bosphorus

formerly used by Turkey's founding president, Kemal Atatürk.
F4 Meşrutiyet Caddesi 98–100, Tepebaşı 212-377-4000 Funicular to Tünel

TAKSIM MEYDANI

This vast, traffic-choked square at the top end of Istiklâl Caddesi (▷ 80–81) takes its name from the stone reservoir on its western side. At its heart is the Cumhuriyet (Republic) Monument, designed by Italian sculptor Pietro Canonica in 1928 and depicting Atatürk and other revolutionary leaders.
J2 Taksim Taksim

TOPHANE MEYDANI

Hidden at the back of a small park behind the Nusretiye Mosque, in the shadow of an old cannon foundry, is a row of cafés that are crowded day and night with people smoking *nargiles* (▷ panel, 86). It's a good place to relax after a visit to Istanbul Modern (▷ 78–79).
H5 Tophane

TÜNEL

The square takes its name from the second oldest (and arguably the shortest) underground railway in the world, constructed by French engineers in 1875 to take foreign businessmen from their offices in Karaköy to their homes in Beyoğlu. The ride by funicular takes only 90 seconds—it takes considerably longer to board and disembark—but is fun and easier on the feet than the steep climb.
F5 Funicular to Tünel Tünel

TÜRK MUSEVILERI MÜZESI

www.muze500.com

Housed in the 19th-century Zulfaris synagogue, the Jewish Museum tells the story of five centuries of Jewish life in Istanbul, from the arrival of the first Sephardic Jews in 1492, welcomed by Sultan Beyazıt II after their expulsion from Spain.
F6 Perçemli Sokağı, Karaköy 212-292-6333 Mon–Thu 10–4, Fri, Sun 10–2 Karaköy None Inexpensive

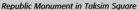

Republic Monument in Taksim Square

An old water tower in Tophane Park

Shopping

ANADOL ANTIK

This Çukurcuma store specializes in wooden cabinets and other antique furniture, but its sidelines include everything from ceramic stoves to chandeliers.

H3 Turnacıbaşı Sokağı 65, Çukurcuma 212-251-5228 Taksim Taksim

ANTIKARNAS

You'll find a wide range of Ottoman antiques and curios on sale at this restored four-story town house in Çukurcuma, as well as various Turkish and European items to browse.

H3 Faik Paşa Yokuşu 15, Çukurcuma 212-251-5928 Taksim Taksim

GÖNÜL PAKSOY

This brilliant designer really is at the cutting edge of Ottoman chic, turning scarves, shawls, slippers and jewelry into works of art through the use of natural fabrics and traditional Ottoman designs.

Off map at J1 Atiye Sokağı 6/A, Teşvikiye 212-236-0209 Teşvikiye, Osmanbey

HOMER

www.homerbooks.com

Turkey's biggest publisher of English-language books has a small shop in Galatasaray selling its own and a range of other titles.

G3 Yeni Çarşı Caddesi 12/A, Galatasaray, Beyoğlu 212-249-5902 Funicular to Tünel

ISTANBUL MÜZIK MERKEZI

This is one of many shops selling musical instruments along Galip Dede Caddesi, a street running down from the Tünel funicular station.

F5 Galip Dede Caddesi 21, Tünel 212-244-5885 Funicular to Tünel

LIBRAIRIE DE PÉRA

Founded in the 1920s, this wonderful antiquarian bookstore and auction house sells maps, prints, engravings, etchings, old photographs and postcards; a treasure trove of memorabilia.

F5 Galip Dede Caddesi 8, Tünel 212-243-7447 Funicular to Tünel

ANTIQUES GALORE

Istanbul probably has more antiques shops per square kilometer than any other European city, selling everything from gorgeous Ottoman furniture to candlesticks. There are at least 85 shops packed into the narrow streets of the Çukurcuma district alone. Alternatively, take the boat to the Sunday market on Ortaköy waterfront, where local artists sell handicrafts and paintings

MAVI JEANS

This popular store is where the city's young and trendy come to get their jeans, as well as denim skirts, T-shirts and accessories.

H2 Istiklal Caddesi 123, Beyoğlu 212-244-6255 Taksim Taksim

MEGAVIZYON

This multimedia megastore has everything from CDs to computer software and books.

H2 Istiklâl Caddesi 57B, Beyoğlu 212-293-0759 Taksim Taksim

PAŞABAHÇE

Turkey's leading glassware manufacturer also owns a retail chain whose biggest branch is on Istiklâl Caddesi.

G4 Istiklâl Caddesi 314, Beyoğlu 212-244-0544 Funicular to Tünel

POPCORN

This curious store specializes in kitsch and off-beat items from c.1950 to yesterday—cameras, clocks, books, old record players and lots more.

H3 Faik Paşa Sokak 2, Çukurcuma 212-249-5859 Taksim Taksim

ROBINSON CRUSOE

A huge bookshop with a good range of English-language titles to browse. The shop also opens on Sundays.

G4 Istiklâl Caddesi 389, Beyoğlu 212-293-6968 Funicular to Tünel

Entertainment and Nightlife

360

www.360istanbul.com

This modern Turkish restaurant on the top floor of a 19th-century apartment block turns into an ultra-trendy bar at night, where a hip crowd sips cocktails on a rooftop terrace with 360-degree views of the city.

G3 Istiklâl Caddesi 309, Beyoğlu 212-251-1042 Daily 6pm–3am Funicular to Tünel

AKBANK SANAT

www.akbanksanat.com

This popular venue for classical music, jazz concerts and films also hosts the Akbank Jazz Festival in October.

H2 Istiklâl Caddesi 14–18, Beyoğlu 212-252-3500 Taksim Taksim

BABYLON

www.babylon.com.tr

Istanbul's premier venue for live rock, jazz and world music, including big-name international stars. In July and August it opens only for occasional special events, as the clubbing scene moves out-of-doors to the Bosphorus shore.

F4 Şehbender Sokağı 3, Tünel 212-292-7368 Tue–Sat 9.30pm–2am; box office 12–9 Funicular to Tünel

BADEHANE

This busy bar, located near the Tünel funicular, is so pupular that it spills out onto the street in summer. It makes a good place for a drink at any time, but the atmosphere is liveliest on Wednesday evening, when gipsy musicians often play here.

F4 General Yazgan Sokağı 5, Tünel 212-249-0550 Daily 9am–2am Funicular to Tünel

CEMAL REŞIT REY KONSER SALONU

This attractive concert hall regularly hosts recitals of classical and Ottoman chamber music.

Off map at J1 Gümüş Sokağı, Harbiye 212-232-9830 Box office daily 10–7.30 Harbiye

DENIZ PALAS

www.iksv.org

www.salonisksv.com

Since 2010, this beautifully restored early 20th-century building has been the HQ of Istanbul Foundation for Culture and Arts (IKSV), which coordinates the city's five major international festivals. Open to visitors, it boasts a café, restaurant (Turkish fusion), design store and its own performance space, Salon.

F4 Sadi Konuralp Caddesi 5, Şişhane 212-334-0733 (center); 212-334-0845 (Salon box office and restaurant) Salon box office Mon–Fri 10–6; restaurant daily 11.30am–2am (reservations essential) Şişhane

GALATA MEVLEVIHANESI

This Sufi monastery and dervish lodge near the Galata Tower is the best place to see the mystical whirling dervish ceremony known as the *Sema*, which is usually held on alternate Sunday afternoons. Tickets are limited and sell quickly, so it is worth buying them from the monastery in advance.

F5 Galip Dede Caddesi 15, Tünel 212-245-4141 Sun 5pm Funicular to Tünel

NARGILES

Once the preserve of wizened old men in cafés, the *nargile* (water-cooled tobacco pipe) has seen a revival in recent years and fashionable young people now puff away at these strange contraptions, with their glass bottles, metal pipes, detachable mouthpieces and glowing coals. Most people opt for apple-scented tobacco but some places offer everything from pistachio to cappuccino. Various *nargile* joints have sprung up behind the Nusretiye Mosque, at Tophane, where Istanbul's bright young things smoke hookahs and lounge leisurely on cushions late into the night.

GALATA TOWER

On the ninth floor of one of Istanbul's most famous landmarks, there are great views of the city by night as you watch the cabaret and belly-dancing show.

F5 Galata Meydanı, Tünel 212-293-8180 Mon–Sat 8pm–midnight Funicular to Tünel

KERVANSARAY

Expensive and theatrical, the dinner show has a live orchestra and voluptuous belly-dancers, plus the chance to have your photo taken dressed as an Ottoman sultan or sultana. Ask for a free shuttle from your hotel when you book your tickets.

Off map at J1 Cumhuriyet Caddesi 30, Harbiye 212-247-1630 Daily 7.30pm Taksim Taksim

KEVE

Upscale bar-café in a 19th-century arcade opposite the upper exit of the Tünel funicular, among old-fashioned street lamps and potted plants—a great place for an early-evening or late-night drink.

F4 Tünel Geçidi 10, Tünel 212-251-4338 Daily 8am–2am Funicular to Tünel

MUNZUR

Munzur is one of a handful of late-night bars along Hasnün Galip Sokağı specializing in Anatolian folk music, with an emphasis on the *bağlama* or *saz* (mandolin). There is no admission charge but tips are expected and drinks are more expensive than elsewhere.

H3 Hasnün Galip Sokağı 21A, Beyoğlu 212-245-4669 Daily 6pm–3am Taksim Taksim

NARDIS

www.nardisjazz.com

In a medieval cellar, located near to the Galata Tower, Nardis is a super-cool, smoky jazz club which attracts at hip crowd and makes for a great night out on the town.

F5 Galata Kulesi Sokağı 14, Tünel 212-244-6327 Mon–Thu 9pm–1am, Fri, Sat 10pm–2am Funicular to Tünel

WHIRLING DERVISHES

The Sufi tradition of whirling dervishes, in which dancers reach a state of spiritual ecstasy through trance-like music and movement, originated in the Turkish city of Konya during the 13th century. The whirling usually takes place during the mystical *Sema* ceremony, and is accompanied by chanting and music on the reed flute, zither and drums. The best place to see it is at Galata Mevlevihanesi (▷ 86). Although the whirling dervishes have become a popular tourist attraction, it is important to remember that this is primarily a religious ceremony.

NARGILEM

One of a long row of places serving tea and *nargiles* to a late-night crowd behind the Nusretiye Mosque in Tophane.

H5 Necatibey Caddesi, Tophane 212-244-2492 Daily 24 hours Tophane

ROXY

The only serious rival to Babylon (▷ 86) as a live music venue, attracting a young crowd with its hip-hop electronic and dance music. Closed from July to September.

J3 Arslan Yatağı Sokağı 7, Beyoğlu 212-249-1283 Wed–Sat 10pm–4am Taksim Taksim

SUREYYA OPERASI

www.sureyyaoperasi.org

This purpose-built theater and opera house, dating from the 1920s, is home to Istanbul State Opera and Ballet. Since a major refurbishment in 2007, it is also a major venue for a superb program of festival events, art exhibitions, concerts and recitals.

Off map Bahariye Caddesi Caferağa Mahallesi 29, Kadıköy 216-346-1531 Box office daily 10–6 Kadıköy

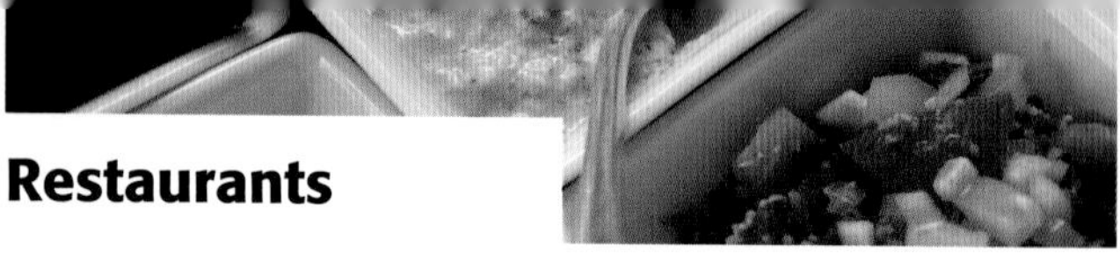

Restaurants

PRICES

Prices are approximate, based on a three-course meal for one person.

€€€ over 50 TL
€€ 30–50 TL
€ under 30 TL

ASMALIMESCIT BALIKÇISI (€€)

On a busy *meyhane* strip near Tünel station, this well-known fish restaurant features live music, regular art exhibitions and a wide-ranging menu of grilled fish, seafood and fishy *mezes*.
F4 Sofyalı Sokağı 5, Tünel 212-251-3939 Mon–Fri 12–2, 6–12, Sat–Sun 6–12 Funicular to Tünel

BONCUK (€€)

Enjoy delicious Armenian and Turkish *mezes*, including aubergine (eggplant) purée, cucumber with yoghurt, and samphire in lemon and olive oil, all washed down with *rakı* at tables on the street.
G3 Nevizade Sokağı 19, Galatarasay 212-243-1219 Daily 12–12 Taksim Taksim

COOKING ALATURKA (€)

www.cookingalaturka.com
Tucked away among the carpet shops, this cooking school and restaurant focuses on vegetarian dishes and Ottoman classics, using locally sourced fresh ingredients.
Off map at J4 Akbiyik Caddesi, 72a Sultahahmet 212-458-5919 Mon–Sat 1pm–3pm, 7.30pm–late Funicular to Tünel

FICCIN (€–€€)

www.ficcin.com
With premises on both sides of the street, Ficcin is popular on account of its relaxed vibe and selection of soups, *mezes* and Caucasian-style Turkish dishes, including *manti* (stuffed pastries).
F6 Galata Caddesi, Sokağı 15/61 212-458-1861 Tue–Sun 12–12 Funicular to Tünel

MEYHANES

A *meyhane* is a tavern where people go to eat *mezes*, invariably washed down by large amounts of *rakı*. Waiters dash around bearing huge trays of *mezes* from which diners make their choice. Although most *meyhanes* also serve grilled meat and fish, it is quite normal to order enough appetizers for everyone to share and skip the main course. These places are particularly good for vegetarians as there is a wide range of options. The liveliest *meyhanes* are in Beyoğlu, on Sofyalı Sokağı near the Tünel funicular and Nevizade Sokağı, half-way up Istiklâl Caddesi.

GALATA EVI (€€)

www.thegalatahouse.com
In a former jail below the Galata Tower, this unusual restaurant has been converted by a husband-and-wife team of architects, and now serves Russian and Georgian cuisine, such as beetroot soup, lamb stew with plums, goulash and potato dumplings.
F6 Galata Kulesi Sokağı 15/61, Tünel 212-245-1861 Tue–Sun 12–12 Funicular to Tünel

HACI ABDULLAH (€€)

www.haciabdullah.com.tr
The oldest and best of Istanbul's *lokantas*, offering ready-prepared dishes such as *imam bayildi* and stuffed vegetables, plus grilled meat and kebabs in a side street off Istiklâl Caddesi. No alcohol.
H2 Sakızağacı Caddesi 9A/17, Beyoğlu 212-293-8561 Daily 12–10.30 Taksim Taksim

IMROZ (€€)

www.krependekiimroz.com
One of the most popular places along the busiest restaurant strip in town, Imroz heaves with diners tucking into well-prepared platters of *mezes* and grilled fish on weekend evenings.
G3 Nevizade Sokağı 24, Galatarasay 212-249-9073 Daily 12–12 Taksim Taksim

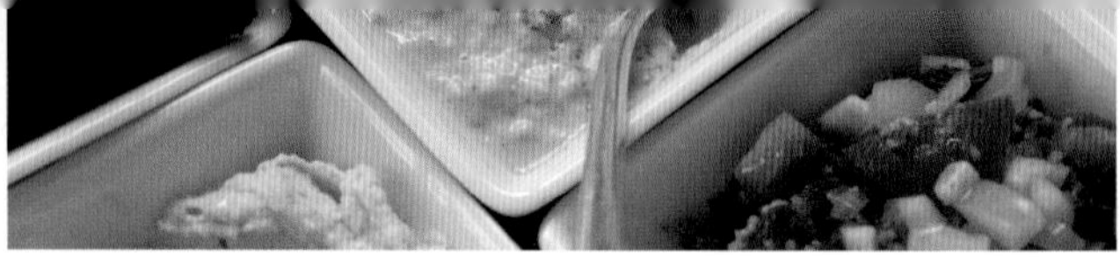

LOKANTA (€€€)

www.lokantadaneve.com
Enjoy funky Turkish-Mediterranean fusion cuisine in a Manhattan-style loft space with exposed brick walls. In summer the restaurant moves upstairs to the Nu Teras rooftop terrace.
F4 Meşrutiyet Caddesi 149, Tepebaşı 212-245-6070 Daily 12–3, 7–4am Funicular to Tünel

MADO (€)

This popular chain outlet sells the best ice cream in Istanbul, made from 100 percent goat's milk with varieties that include chocolate, pistachio and sour cherry.
G3 Istiklâl Caddesi 186/2, Beyoğlu 212-244-1781 Daily 9am–1am Funicular to Tünel

MIKLA (€€€)

www.miklarestaurant.com
On the top floors of the Marmara Pera Hotel, Mikla is the latest project of Turko-Finnish chef Mehmet Gürs, who is pushing back the boundaries of modern Turkish cuisine with new-wave Mediterranean and Scandinavian creations. In summer, there are outdoor terraces and a cool rooftop cocktail bar and pool.
F4 Meşrutiyet Caddesi 167–185, Tepebaşı 212-293-5656 Daily noon–2am Funicular to Tünel

NEYLE MEYLE (€€)

www.neylemeyle.com
Seafood, grilled fish and vegetarian *mezes* are all on the menu at this lively and popular *meyhane*.
G3 Nevizade Sokağı 12, Galatarasay 212-249-8103 Daily 12–12 Taksim Taksim

OTANTIK (€)

Women in Anatolian costume make gözleme (pancakes) in the window of this rustic restaurant, which serves cheap, filling Anatolian dishes such as potato dumplings, casseroles and pancakes.
G3 Istiklâl Caddesi 170, Beyoğlu 212-293-8451 Daily 9am–10pm Funicular to Tünel

RAKI

The national drink of Turkey, *rakı,* is distilled from sweet raisins, with anise added. The word derives from the Arabic *araki* ('sweating'), a reference to the distilling process. Most Turks drink *rakı* mixed with ice and water, which turns it a milky hue—it is referred to colloquially as the 'lion's milk'. *Rakı* production became a state monopoly in the 1930s and it was privatized only in 2004. The most popular variety of the drink, Yeni Rakı, is 45 percent proof.

PALMIYE (€€)

www.palmiyerestaurant.com
In the famous 'Flower Passage' (Çiçek Pasaji, ▷ 82), try *mezes*, meat and fish dishes.
G3 Çiçek Pasaji, Galatasaray 212-249-2101 Daily 11am–midnight Taksim Taksim

REFIK (€€)

The oldest of the *meyhanes* in the Tünel district features mostly fish dishes, as well as *mezes* and salads.
F4 Sofyalı Sokağı 10, Tünel 212-243-2834 Mon–Sat 12–12, Sun 6pm–midnight Funicular to Tünel

SOFYALI 9 (€€)

www.sofyali.com
This busy tavern offers *mezes* and grills in a lovely old house in Tünel. Arrive early or come late if you want a table out on the street.
F4 Sofyalı Sokağı 9, Tünel 212-245-0362 Mon–Sat 12–12 Funicular to Tünel

VENTA DEL TORO (€€)

If you need a break from Turkish cuisine, try this Spanish-style tapas bar beside the Galata Tower offering paella, tortilla, ham and other Spanish classics as well as 'Turkish tapas'.
F5 Galip Dede Caddesi 145, Tünel 212-243-6049 Daily 11am–2am Funicular to Tünel

Farther Afield

You can't fully experience Istanbul without taking to the water, on the ferries that cross the Bosphorus between the Asian and European shores, passing decadent Ottoman palaces built by the sultans during the dying days of empire.

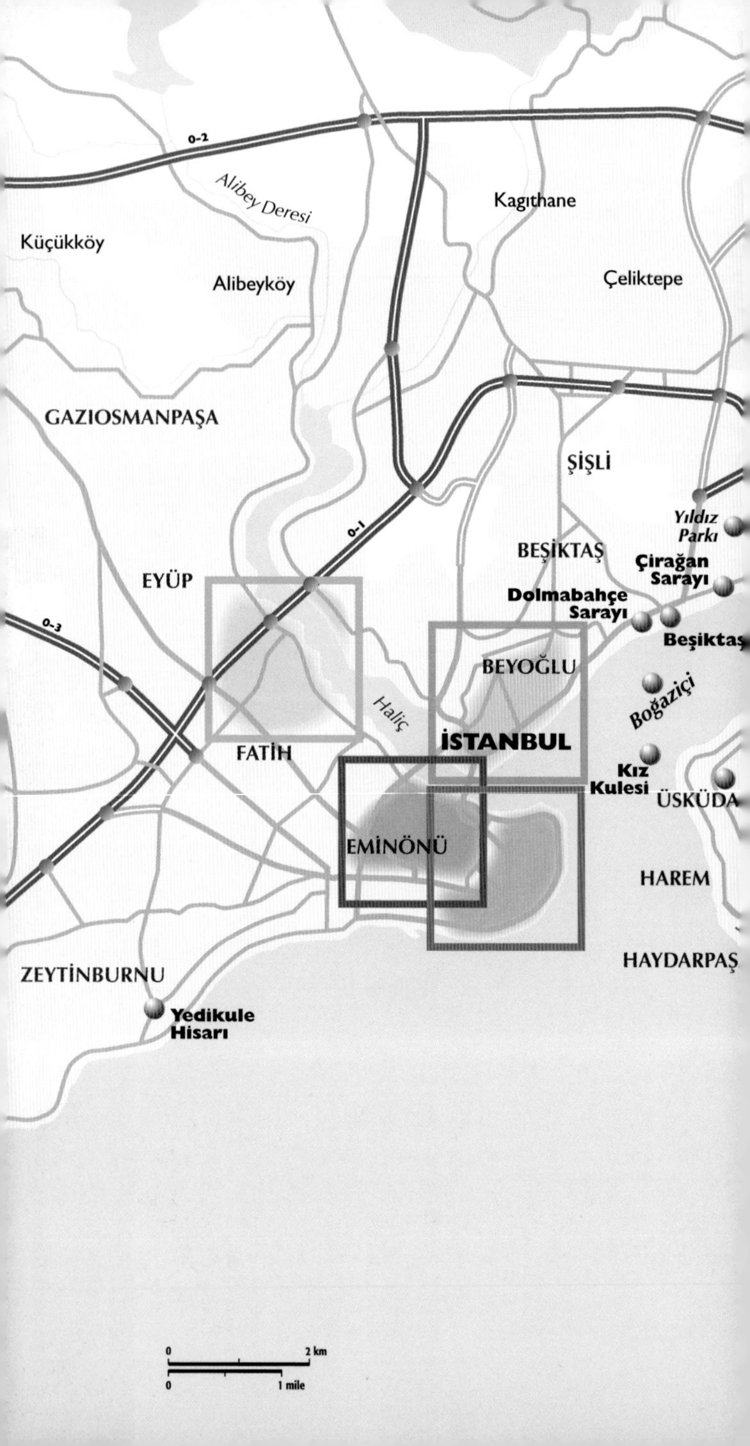

0-2
Alibey Deresi
Kagıthane
Küçükköy
Alibeyköy
Çeliktepe
GAZIOSMANPAŞA
ŞİŞLİ
0-1
Yıldız
Parkı
BEŞİKTAŞ
Çirağan
Sarayı
EYÜP
Dolmabahçe
Sarayı
0-3
Beşiktaş
BEYOĞLU
Haliç
Boğaziçi
İSTANBUL
FATİH
Kız
Kulesi
ÜSKÜDA
EMİNÖNÜ
HAREM
HAYDARPAŞ
ZEYTİNBURNU
Yedikule
Hisarı
0
2 km
0
1 mile

İstinye
Sadberk Hanım Müzesi
Sakıp Sabancı Müzesi
Anadolu Kavağı
Çubuklu
Kanlıca
Rumeli Hisarı
Anadolu Hisarı
Levent
Bebek
Göksu Deresi
O-2
Kandilli
Arnavutköy
Vaniköy
Çengelköy
Ortaköy
BEYLERBEYİ
Beylerbeyi Sarayı
O-1
Büyük Çamlıca
Bulgurlu
Ümraniye
O-1
KADMODA
Kadıköy
KIZILTOPRAK
FENERBAHÇE
İstanbul Oyuncak Müzesi
ERENKÖY
Fener Burun
Bostancı

Beylerbeyi Sarayı

TOP 25

Exterior view (left); a chandelier and ornate decoration inside (right)

THE BASICS

- Off map to east
- Abdullah Ağa Caddesi
- 216-321-9320
- Tue, Wed, Fri–Sun 9.30–4
- Café (€)
- 15 from Üsküdar
- None
- Moderate
- Guided tours only. Photographs can be taken in grounds only

HIGHLIGHTS

- Empress Eugénie's room
- Bronze horse in grounds
- Terrace garden
- Harem waterfront gate
- Rush-matting floors
- Rope motif furniture in Admiral's sitting room
- Pool salon
- Wooden staircase linking *harem* with *selamlık*
- Blue reception room
- Wood panels
- Prayer room with rugs
- Abdülaziz's reinforced bed

You arrive at Beylerbeyi Palace to the beguiling sounds of Asian music, transmitted through speakers concealed among the magnolias of the terrace garden. Before the guided tour begins, admire the views across to Ortaköy.

French empress This attractive summer palace was built for Sultan Abdülaziz in 1861. Its most celebrated occupant was Empress Eugénie of France, wife of Napoleon III, who stayed here in 1869 en route to opening the Suez Canal. Abdülaziz is said to have become infatuated with her after attending the Paris exhibition two years earlier, and went to immense trouble to make her visit enjoyable.

The palace Comprising just 24 rooms and six salons, divided into the traditional *selamlık* and *harem*, Beylerbeyi is more modest, though no less luxurious than Dolmabahçe (▷ 96–97). To keep the apartments cool in summer, all the floors were covered with rush mats, and a recessed marble pool and fountain were built into the floor of the pool salon—one of the most impressive rooms in the palace. Abdülaziz was a keen sailor, and in the Admiral's sitting room all the furniture is ingeniously carved with rope motifs. Visitors are also shown Empress Eugénie's suite, with its specially Westernized bathroom, the Sultan's prayer room and the 2m-long (6.5ft) bed reinforced to accommodate his enormous frame—he was a formidable wrestler!

A boat trip on the Bosphorus should be on every visitor's must-do list

TOP 25 Boğaziçi (Bosphorus)

One of Istanbul's most memorable experiences is to sail out onto the Bosphorus, passing fishing villages, medieval fortresses, sumptuous Ottoman palaces and shuttered *yalıs* (wooden mansions).

Ford of the ox The Bosphorus is a narrow stretch of water about 30km (18.5 miles) long, which threads its way from the Sea of Marmara to the Black Sea, forming a natural barrier between Europe and Asia. Bosphorus means 'ford of the ox' and derives from the Greek myth of Io. While being hotly pursued by Hera, wife of Zeus, Io is turned into an ox and in that guise escapes across the strait. Today the Bosphorus is spanned by two road bridges.

Ports of call The cheapest way to see the Bosphorus is to take the ferry—there are daily departures from the pier at Eminönü, beside the Galata Bridge. There are several stops en route. Kanlıca is famous for its yoghurt, served with jam, sugar or honey in the square behind the pier. Yeniköy has splendid art nouveau mansions lining the waterfront. Sarıyer is known for its fishing fleet, while at Kilyos (a short bus ride away) you can swim in the Black Sea. Before returning to Istanbul, the ferry ties up for three hours at Anadolu Kavağı, giving you time to climb the hill to the Genoese castle, or lunch in a waterfront restaurant. If you return on the later ferry there's the bonus of a beautiful sunset as you approach the city.

THE BASICS

www.ido.com.tr

Departures from Eminönü: F8

212-444-4436

Departures daily at 10.35; also at 12 and 1.35 mid-Jun to mid-Sep

Fish restaurants at Sarıyer and Anadolu Kavağı

Eminönü, Beşiktaş, Kanlıca, Yeniköy, Sarıyer, Anadolu Kavağı

None

Expensive

HIGHLIGHTS

- Dolmabahçe Sarayı (▷ 96)
- Ortaköy Camii (▷ 100)
- Beylerbeyı Sarayı (▷ 94)
- Rumeli Hisarı (▷ 101)
- Anadolu Kavağı (▷ 99)
- Wooden mansions (*yalıs*)
- Kanlıca yoghurt
- Sadberk Hanim Müzesi (▷ 101)

Dolmabahçe Sarayı

TOP 25

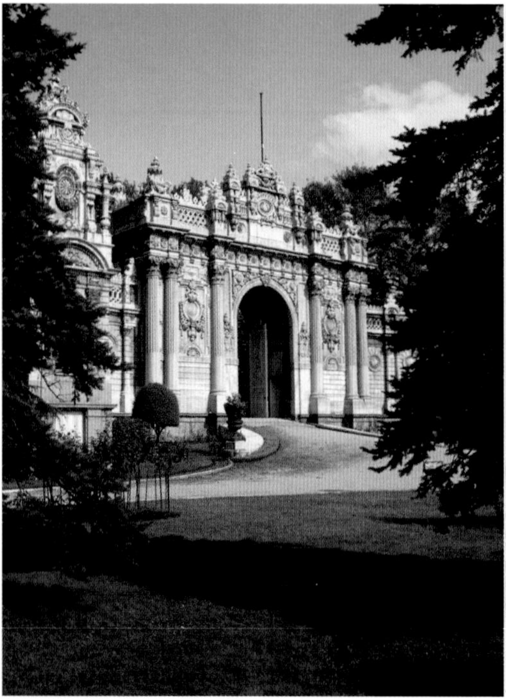

HIGHLIGHTS

- Marble facade
- Throne Room
- Ceremonial staircase
- Sultan's bathroom
- Atatürk's bedroom
- Clock stopped at exact time of Atatürk's death

TIP

- To see more palace treasures, visit the Depo Müze (Depot Museum), a vast Ottoman junk shop in the former palace kitchens at Beşiktaş.

Although the taste of the builders of Dolmabahçe Palace might be subject to doubt, the building's entertainment value lies in the sheer extravagance of its interiors—a relentless accumulation of ostentatious luxury and rococo excess.

A new palace By far the most sumptuous of the sultans' palaces, Dolmabahçe stands on the site of a reclaimed port—the Turkish word means 'filled-in garden'. It was commissioned by Sultan Abdülmecit from the architects Karabet Balyan and his son, Nikoğos, in 1843, and the royal entourage moved here from Topkapı 13 years later. The palace was so expensive, it contributed in part to the bankrupting of the Ottoman treasury in 1881. The first President of the Republic, Mustafa

It's certainly not plain—the sumptuous Dolmabahçe Palace helped to bankrupt the Ottoman treasury in 1881

Kemal Atatürk, stayed in Dolmabahçe in 1927, rechristening it the Palace of the Nation. He died here on 10 November 1938 during a visit.

Interiors The layout preserves the traditional division between *selamlık* (state rooms) and harem (private apartments). Separating the two is the largest throne room in the world, its trompe-l'oeil ceiling supported by 56 Corinthian columns. It was here that the first Ottoman parliament was convened in 1877. Other highlights include the magnificent formal staircase, with a balustrade of Baccarat crystal and the Hünkar Hamamı (Sultan's bathroom), with walls of alabaster imported from Egypt. The decoration is almost exclusively Western, after a style the French novelist, Théophile Gautier, described ironically as 'Louis XIV orientalisé'.

THE BASICS

www.dolmabahce.gov.tr
Off map to northeast
Dolmabahçe Caddesi, Beşiktaş
212-236-9000
Tue–Wed, Fri–Sun 9–4
Kabataş
None
Expensive (extra charge for photography)
Allow 2 hours for a visit; guided tours only

Yıldız Parkı

TOP 25

Yıldız Şale (left) and the Grand Room (middle); a bandstand in the park (right)

THE BASICS

- Off map to northeast
- Çırağan Caddesi, between Beşiktaş and Ortaköy
- Yıldız Şale: 212-259-4570
- Park: daily 9–6. Yıldız Şale: Tue, Wed, Fri–Sun 9.30–5 in summer, 9.30–4 in winter
- Cafés (€) and Malta Kiosk (€€€)
- 25E from Kabataş
- Beşiktaş
- None
- Park: free. Yıldız Şale: moderate
- Yıldız Şale guided tours only

HIGHLIGHTS

Park
- Malta Kiosk
- Yıldız Porcelain Factory
- Shady parks and gardens

Yıldız Şale
- Ceremonial hall
- Hereke carpet (400sq m/ 478sq yards)
- Banqueting room

The last of the great Ottoman palaces, Yıldız Şarayı, is mainly popular for its stunning grounds, Yıldız Park.

Yıldız Parkı In a city with so much traffic and noise, green space is at a premium and when the people of Istanbul need to breathe, they come to Yıldız Park. On weekend afternoons, families picnic and lovers stroll in this magnificent 50ha (123-acre) park, scented with orange blossom, on a wooded hillside above the Bosphorus. The park was used as an imperial estate in the reign of Sultan Ahmet (1603–17), though the pavilions and kiosks date from the late-19th century. Among the buildings here are the Çadir Kiosk, now a pleasant lakeside café; Malta Kiosk, a smart restaurant with a terrace overlooking the river; and Yıldız Porcelain Factory (▷ 104), built to provide china for the palace kitchens and still in use today.

Yıldız Şale Sultan Abdülhamid II commissioned the hilltop palace in 1875 because it was thought to be more secure from attack than Dolmabahçe (▷ 96–97). It turned out to be the last of the Ottoman palaces to be built in Istanbul. In addition to the palace, Yıldız Şale, at the top of the park, was originally built as a guesthouse to accommodate royal visitors to the palace, but later became the sultan's chief residence. Designed to resemble a Swiss chalet, its 64 rooms contain an intriguing blend of baroque and Islamic styles.

More to See

ANADOLU HISARI

This castle, on the Asian shore of the Bosphorus beneath Fatih Bridge, was begun in 1390 by Sultan Beyazıt I. The barbican and towers were added by Mehmet II just before the city's conquest in 1453. The 'Fortress of Anatolia' is closed to visitors, but it is impressive from the outside and is only a short walk from the pseudo-baroque palace of Küçüksu Kasrı.

Off map to northeast Körfez Caddesi, Kanlıca Café (€) nearby 15 from Üsküdar

ANADOLU KAVAĞI

The final stop on the Bosphorus ferry is a busy Asian fishing village, with restaurants by the port catering for the large number of day-trippers. A steep climb out of the village leads to Yoros Castle, a ruined Genoese fortress of Byzantine origin, whose clifftop setting offers great views of the Bosphorus and Black Sea.

Off map to northeast Lots of restaurants (€–€€€) Anadolu Kavağı

BEŞIKTAŞ

Shortly after passing the white marble facade of Dolmabahçe Palace, the Bosphorus ferry makes its first stop, at Beşiktaş. You can watch the passengers disembark at the elegant art nouveau jetty, sip tea in waterside cafés, stroll along the promenade or visit the Deniz Müzesi (Naval Museum).

Off map to northeast Naval Museum: Wed–Sun 9–4 Cafés (€) and restaurants (€€) Beşiktaş

BÜYÜK ÇAMLICA

Climb 'Great Pine Mountain' at the highest point of the city (268m/879ft) to look over the Golden Horn and Sea of Marmara.

Off map to east Büyükçamlıca Tepesi Café and teahouse (€) Üsküdar, then taxi Free

ÇIRAĞAN SARAYI

This stately waterfront palace was commissioned by Sultan Abdülaziz and completed in 1874. His successor, Murat V, was confined here

Ferries moored at the quayside at Beşiktaş

Climb to Yoros Castle, at Anadolu Kavağı, for great views

for more than 30 years after he was deposed in 1876. The palace was destroyed by fire in 1910 and has been restored and reopened as a luxury hotel (▷ 112).
Off map to northeast Çırağan Caddesi 32, Beşiktaş 212-326-4646 Beşiktaş

ISTANBUL OYUNCAK MÜZESI
www.istanbuloyuncakmuzesi.com
The Istanbul Toy Museum has a charming collection of antique toys. Weekend puppet and magic shows.
Off map to southeast Ömerpaşa Caddesi Dr Zeki Zeren Sokak 17, Göztepe 216-359-4550 Tue–Sun 9.30–6 Café (€) Göztepe Bus from Kadiköy to Göztepe Moderate

KADIKÖY
Regular ferries from Eminönü take foot passengers to this busy shopping area on the Asian side, on the site of the ancient Greek city of Chalcedon. On the way there are magnificent views.
Off map to southeast Kadiköy

KIZ KULESI
www.kizkulesi.com.tr/en
The 18th-century Kız Kulesi (Maiden's Tower or Leander's Tower) is on an island at the entrance to the Bosphorus. You can take a boat trip to the tower and restaurant from Kabataş or Salacak (ferry to Üsküdar and walk along the promenade).
Off map to east 216-342-4747 Daily 9–6.45, (8pm–midnight with reservation) Restaurant (€€€) Boat trip: moderate Salacak: daily 9–6.45, 8.15–12.30; Kabataş: daily 9–6.45 every hour, then 8pm, 8.45pm, 9.30pm

ORTAKÖY
With the beautiful Ortaköy Camii reflected in the Bosphorus under the mighty Atatürk Bridge, Ortaköy is one of the most attractive spots in Istanbul. The square by the port is lined with fish restaurants; on Sunday morning the lanes come alive with an arts and crafts market.
Off map to northeast Cafés (€) and restaurants (€€) 25E, 40 Ortaköy

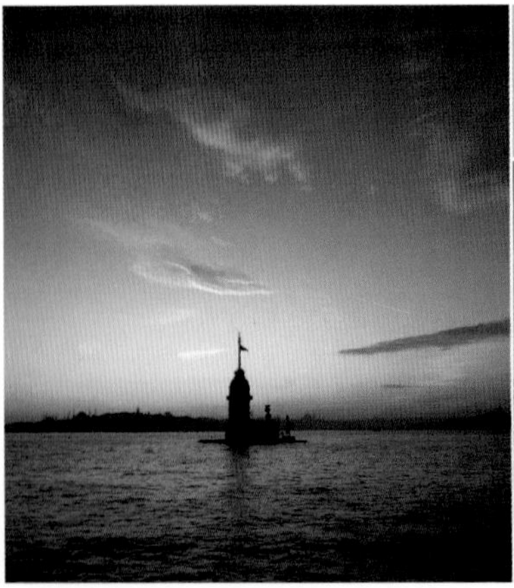

The Maiden's Tower guards the entrance to the Bosphorus

Ortaköy Camii, near Atatürk Bridge

RUMELI HISARI

This superb fortress was built in 1452 by Mehmet II. You can explore the walls and garden terraces, and, in summer, attend a concert at the open-air arena.

Off map to northeast Yahya Kemal Caddesi 42, Rumeli Hisarı 212-263-5305 Thu–Tue 9–12, 12.30–4.30 25E, 40 None Inexpensive

SADBERK HANIM MÜZESI

www.sadberkhanimmuzesi.org.tr

This private museum, a short walk south of the ferry dock at Sarıyer, has two wings. The first is devoted to archaeology, with items from Anatolian, Roman and Byzantine cultures dating from 5000BC. The second features Turkish arts, crafts and ethnography, with displays of Iznik tiles, embroidered costumes and an exhibition on marriage, child-birth and circumcision customs.

Off map to northeast Büyükdere Piyası Caddesi 27–29, Sarıyer 212-242-3813 Thu–Tue 10–5 Tea garden (€) Moderate Sarıyer

SAKIP SABANCI MÜZESI

http://muze.sabanciuniv.edu

This museum is worth visiting not only for the 1920s villa with its 18th/19th-century furnishings and Bosphorus views, but for the outstanding international exhibitions and the permanent collection tracing five centuries of the art of calligraphy.

Off map to northeast Sakıp Sabancı Caddesi 42, Emirgân 212-227-2200 Tue, Thu–Sun 10–6, Wed 10–10 Winter Garden café (€€), Müzedechnaga (▷ 106) 25E (direction Sarıyer), 40 from Taksim to Sarıyer Kabataş Good Moderate

ÜSKÜDAR

Ferries cross the Bosphorus from Eminönü to Üsküdar at approximately 20-minute intervals. Take a closer look at the elaborate fountain, built by Sultan Ahmet III in memory of his mother, and then at the Mihrimar Sultan Mosque opposite the jetty.

Off map to east Üsküdar

The Ottoman-style facade of the Sadberk Hanim Müzesi

Rumeli Hisari was built by Mehmet II in four months for the siege of Constantinople

Excursions

THE BASICS

Distance: 20km (12.5 miles)

Journey time: 40–50 minutes

Ferry to Büyükada departs daily 9.30am, 10am and 11.30am; last return ferry 10pm. Note: if you buy a return ticket you can't island hop. To ensure a seat, get onboard 30 minutes prior to departure

Seafront restaurants at Büyükada. Botanik (▷ 105) is among the best

Kabataş

Pony and trap rides cost 50–60 TL for long or short tours

Museum of the Princes' Islands

Adalar Müzesi Hangar Müze Binası, Aya Nikola Mevkii, Büyükada

216-382-5280/216-382-6430

Tue–Sun summer 10–7, winter 10–6

Inexpensive

KIZIL ADALAR (PRINCES' ISLANDS)

This archipelago off the Asian coast of the Sea of Marmara is Istanbul's most popular resort, and the ferries are crowded on summer weekends with day-trippers and picnicking families.

Ferries call at four islands—Burguzada, Heybeliada, Kınalıada and Büyükada, though only the last two are of real interest to visitors. The archipelago takes its English name from the unfortunate Byzantine princes who were exiled here in days gone by. In the late-19th century, steamers brought day-trippers and longer-term summer residents who built the handsome villas visitors see today.

First stop is Kınalıada (40 minutes), where the main attraction is the narrow stony beach with its waterfront restaurants. If swimming isn't your thing, then stay on board for the extra 10 minutes to Büyükada (the largest island) where there's more to see and do. Motorized traffic is banned everywhere on the archipelago but you can get around easily enough by hiring a bicycle, taking a boat trip, or riding in a pony and trap (long and short tours, departing from the Clock Tower). The most popular destination is Ayos Georgios (St. George's Monastery), which you can reach in under an hour on foot. While there's little left of this sixth-century foundation apart from the chapel, the panoramic views are well worth the climb and there's a restaurant serving lunch if you haven't brought a picnic.

A new attraction on Büyükada is the Museum of the Princes' Islands, which opened in September 2010 in a converted helicopter hangar at Aya Nikola. Through touch screens, videos and old recordings you learn all about the formation of the islands, popular culture and the environment, as well as the issues that concern the islanders today. You can find out more about Büyükada's attractions from the information office next to the old ferry terminal.

Shopping

AKMERKEZ
www.akmerkez.co.tr
The biggest and best of the American-style shopping malls springing up in the city, this has chains such as Benetton and Zara, designer clothes from Vakko, plus jewelers, book and music stores, a cinema and restaurants. To get there, take the metro from Taksim Square.
Off map Nispetiye Caddesi, Etiler 212-282-0170 Levent

KANYON
www.kanyon.com.tr
This shopping mall has won architectural awards for its design, with open-air corridors around a dramatic interior canyon. There is a flagship branch of Harvey Nichols, together with local and global fashion brands, cinemas and restaurants.
Off map Büyükdere Caddesi 185, Levent 212-317-5300 Levent

DAMAS
Shop in the luxurious surroundings of the shopping arcade at the Çırağan Palace hotel (▷ 112), which includes a fantastic jewelry showroom featuring exclusive designer names, precious metal and gemstone products.
Off map Çırağan Caddesi 32, Beşiktaş 212-259-8795 Beşiktaş

YILDIZ PORSELEN FABRIKASI
Located just beside the entrance to the red-brick factory, in the grounds of Yıldız Park (▷ 98), is a small shop selling famous home-produced porcelain, which make ideal gifts to take home.
Off map Yıldız Parkı 212-260-2370 25E from Kabataş Beşiktaş

Entertainment and Nightlife

REINA
www.reina.com.tv
Famous summertime megaclub on the banks of the Bosphorus, where Istanbul's celebrities and wannabes hang out on balmy nights.
Off map Muallim Naci Caddesi, Ortaköy 212-259-5919 Jun–Sep daily 7pm–4am

SOCCER
Most male Turks are passionate about soccer and the three biggest teams (Beşiktaş, Fenerbahçe and Galatasaray) all play in Istanbul. Beşiktaş play at the Inönü stadium, close to Dolmabahçe Palace; Galatasaray at the new Turk Telecom Arena at Seyrantepe in the north of the city; and Fenerbahçe at the şükrü Saracoğlu stadium in Kadıköy, which hosted the 2009 UEFA Cup final. Most league matches take place on weekends from August to May, with European fixtures midweek. Tickets go on sale a few days beforehand, at the stadiums and at Biletix outlets.
Beşiktaş: www.bjk.com.tr 212-310-1000
Fenerbahçe: www.fenerbahce.org 216-542-1907
Galatasaray: www.galatasaray.org 212-216-1500

TURKISH GRAND PRIX

Istanbul became a new name on the Formula One circuit in 2005 when it hosted the Turkish Grand Prix at the Istanbul Park race track in Tuzla, close to Sabiha Gökçen Airport, in front of a sell-out crowd of 125,000 spectators. The Turkish Grand Prix is now a regular event on the motor-racing calendar.

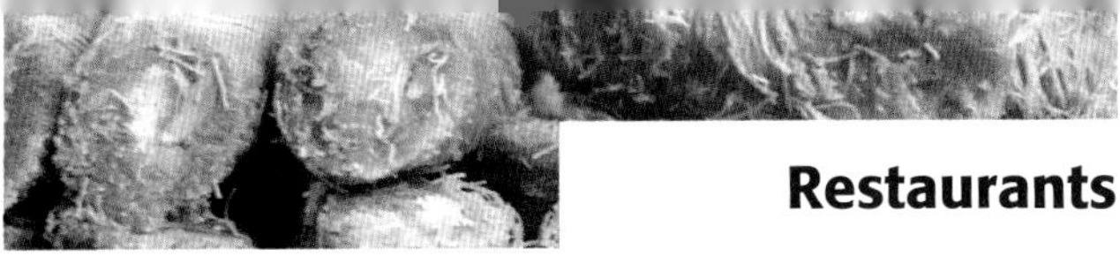

Restaurants

PRICES

Prices are approximate, based on a three-course meal for one person.

€€€	more than 50 TL
€€	30–50 TL
€	under 30 TL

A'JIA (€€€)

www.ajiahotel.com

Dreamy terrace views of the Bosphorus are the star attraction of this expensive and beautiful Italian–Mediterranean accented restaurant.

Off map · Çubuklu Caddesi, Kanlıca · 216-413-9353 · Daily 7am–midnight · Kanlıca

AQUARIUS (€€€)

www.aquariusbalik.com

This well-known fish restaurant beside the port at Sarıyer has three floors of seating and an extensive riverside terrace.

Off map · Cami Arkası Sokak 11/13, Sarıyer · 212-271-3434 · Daily 12–12 · Sarıyer

ASIRLIK KANLICA YOĞURDU (€)

The village of Kanlıca is famous for its yoghurt (▷ 95), which you can sample at this waterfront café beside the Bosphorus. Or stay on board to Anadolu Kavağı and pots of yoghurt will be brought to the ferry.

Off map · Iskele Yanı 2, Kanlıca · 216- 413-4469 · Daily 9–9 · Kanlıca

AYA YORGI MANASTIRI (€)

Grilled meat on an outdoor terrace with fabulous views beside St. George's Monastery—a good place to relax after the steep climb.

Off map · Aya Yorgi Manastiri, Büyükada · No phone · Daily 12–9 · Büyükada, Princes' Islands

BABA (€€)

www.kavakbaba.com

Turn left on leaving the ferry at Anadolu Kavağı and walk to the end of the village to reach this attractive fish restaurant, with a terrace right over the water.

Off map · Iskele Caddesi 13, Anadolu Kavağı · 216-320-2047 · Daily 12–12 · Anadolu Kavağı

BANYAN (€€€)

www.banyanrestaurant.com

Stylish Southeast Asian fusion food in a stunning waterfront setting beside the Bosphorus at Ortaköy. Try the Banyan plate for two to share, which includes crispy vegetables, prawns, sushi and spicy dips, followed by lamb satay or steak with teriyaki and almond mash.

Off map · Salhane Sokak 3/2, Ortaköy · 212-259-9060 · Mon–Sat 12–12, Sun 10am–midnight · Ortaköy

ORTAKÖY DINING

Ortaköy (▷ 101), one of Istanbul's most vibrant districts, has a waterfront lined with fantastic little cafés and terrace restaurants that boast superb views of the Bosphorus, as well as of the exquisite 19th-century Ortaköy Mosque. A street market draws the crowds on Sunday, and there are also craft and junk shops just waiting to be explored.

BOTANIK (€€)

Charming waterfront restaurant five minutes left of the jetty. Try the likes of fish soup, stuffed mussels and a delicious octopus casserole.

Off map · Gülistan Caddesi 42, Büyükada · 212-382-3722 · Daily 11–11 · Büyükada, Princes' Islands

ÇINARALTI (€€)

Waterfront restaurant with outdoor tables on the square by the port at Ortaköy, with a wide choice of *mezes* and fresh fish.

Off map · Iskele Meydanı 28, Ortaköy · 212-261-4616 · Daily noon–1am · Ortaköy

DENIZ KIZI (€€)

Intimate, cozy little fish restaurant near the port at Sarıyer, with a handful of outdoor tables under a shady terrace.

Off map · Balıkçılar Çarşısı, Sarıyer · 212-242-8570 · Daily 12–12 · Sarıyer

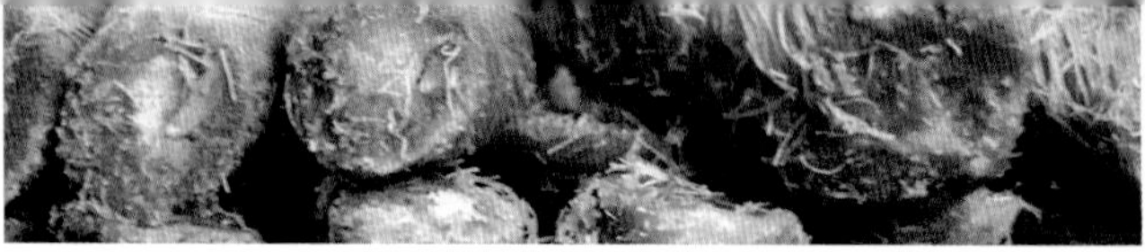

GÖZDE (€€)
You'll spot this three-story restaurant as soon as you step off the ferry and onto the main square. Grilled fish is what it does best.
Off map ✉ Iskele Meydanı, Anadolu Kavağı ☎ 216-320-2568 Daily 12–12 Anadolu Kavağı

KANAAT (€)
Founded in 1933, this large no-frills *lokanta*, a short walk from the ferry dock, serves dishes such as vegetables in olive oil and cucumber with yoghurt, as well as home-made desserts.
Off map ✉ Selmanı Pak Caddesi 25, Üsküdar ☎ 216-341-5444 Daily 9am–11pm Üsküdar

KAVAK DOĞANAY (€€)
www.kavakdoganay.com
The oldest of the fish restaurants in Anadolu Kavağı is in a perfect setting by the port with a waterfront terrace.
Off map ✉ Yalı Caddesi 13, Anadolu Kavağı ☎ 216-320-2036 Daily 12–12 Anadolu Kavağı

MÜZEDECHANGA (€€€)
www.changa-istanbul.com
This restaurant at the Sakıp Sabancı Museum has won plaudits both for its award-winning minimalist design and its refreshing approach to Turkish cooking. The food is infused with the flavors of the Mediterranean under the guidance of Kiwi chef and culinary consultant, Peter Gordon, who devised the menu. In good weather, it's definitely worth booking a table on the terrace. The less expensive Winter Garden café is open during museum hours for snacks.
Off map ✉ Sakıp Sabancı Caddesi 42, Emirgân ☎ 212-323-0901 Tue–Sun 10.30am–1am 25E or 40, direction Sarıyer

RUMELI ISKELE (€€)
www.rumeliiskele.com
Enjoy tasty seafood *mezes* and fish dishes in this popular place near the fortress at Rumeli Hisarı, with fantastic views across the water to Anadolu Hisarı on the far side.
Off map ✉ Yahya Kemal Caddesi 1, Rumeli Hisarı ☎ 212-263-2997 Daily 12–12 25E or 40 to Rumeli Hisarı

FISHERMAN'S CATCH

Balık—fish
Hamsi—anchovy
Istavrit—mackerel
Kalamar—squid
Karides—prawns
Kılıç—swordfish
Levrek—bass
Lüfer—blue fish
Midye—mussels
Palamut/torik—bonito
Tekir—mullet
Yengeç—crab

VOGUE (€€€)
www.voguerestaurant.com
Hang out with the beautiful people at this trendy Beşiktaş restaurant, with a 13th-floor rooftop terrace overlooking the Bosphorus, and a menu that ranges in style from sushi to Turkish-Mediterranean fusion dishes.
Off map ✉ Spor Caddesi 92, Beşiktaş ☎ 212-227-4404 Daily 12–2, 7–2 Beşiktaş

YELKEN (€€€)
www.yelkenrestaurant.com
This pretty waterfront restaurant beside the ferry dock at Yeniköy features superb fish dishes such as stuffed sea bass, paella and seafood spaghetti. In summer, you can eat on a terrace above the water.
Off map ✉ Köybası Caddesi 71, Yeniköy ☎ 212-262-9490 Daily 12–12 Yeniköy

YOROS CAFÉ (€€)
Occupying a series of terraces tumbling down the hillside beneath Yoros Castle, this open-air restaurant serves a simple menu of grilled fish, mussels, chips and salad, with the bonus of some magnificent views over the Bosphorus. Check out the bargain fixed-price lunch.
Off map ✉ Baba Sokak 76, Anadolu Kavağı ☎ 216-320-2028 Daily 12–12 Anadolu Kavağı

Where to Stay

Istanbul has accommodation for all styles and budgets, from inexpensive hostels to five-star hotels. If you want a room with character, stay in a restored Ottoman-era house in Sultanahmet or sleep in a sultan's palace on the Bosphorus shore.

Introduction

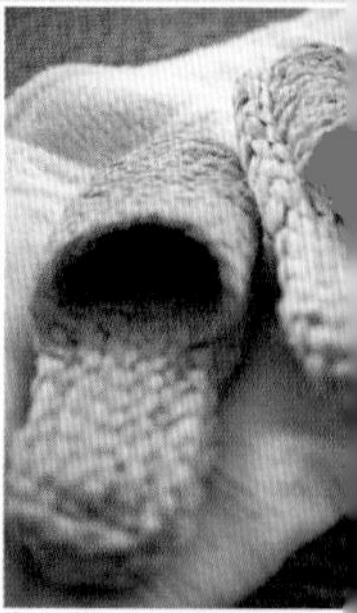

The range of accommodation options is growing all the time, with new apartments, waterfront mansions and boutique hotels. Rooms are at a premium during the summer, so reserve well in advance.

Districts

Most of the budget accommodation is in and around Sultanahmet. There are inexpensive hotels and backpacker hostels on Akbıyık Caddesi. This area also has a large number of 'Ottoman' hotels, in historic wooden houses with roof terraces overlooking the Sea of Marmara. The largest concentration of Ottoman hotels is in the quiet streets around Küçük Ayasofya. Most luxury accommodation is found north of the Golden Horn, in the area around Harbiye and Taksim Square. A recent trend has been the opening of charming chic boutique hotels in restored wooden mansions along the Bosphorus.

Practicalities

The peak season is from May to September, and you should book ahead at this time. Istanbul Hotels (www.istanbulhotels.com) has lists of hotels by type and includes links to the hotels' own websites. Prices are usually quoted in euros, though you can pay in Turkish lira. Most hotels accept credit cards but there may be a discount for paying in cash. The price of a room generally includes a full Turkish breakfast, with pastries, bread, cheese, eggs, olives and tomatoes.

HOTEL CHAINS

The big international hotel chains have branches in Istanbul. Try the Hilton (☎ 212-315-6000; www.hilton.com), Grand Hyatt Istanbul (☎ 212-368-1234; www.istanbul.regency.hyatt.com), Mövenpick (☎ 212-319-2929; www.movenpick-hotels.com), Ritz-Carlton (☎ 212-334-4444; www.ritzcarlton.com) and Swissôtel (☎ 212-326-1100; www.swissotel.com). For longer stays, you could rent an apartment through Istanbul Rentals (☎ 212-638-1215; www.istanbulrentals.com).

Budget Hotels

PRICES

Expect to pay between €40 and €90 per night for a double room in a budget hotel.

ANTIQUE

www.hotelantique.com

Antique is a small, friendly hotel with 17 simply furnished but comfortable rooms on a quiet street near the Arasta Bazaar. In summer, you can take your breakfast on the rooftop terrace.

G12 Oğul Sokağı 17, Sultanahmet 212-516-4936 Sultanahmet

DENIZ HOUSES

www.denizhouses.com

Opened in 2006 by the owners of Sultan's Inn (▷ this page), the 'house of the sea' has 15 rooms in a beautifully restored wooden house in Küçük Ayasofya.

F12 Çayiroğlu Sokağı 14, Sultanahmet 212-518-9595 Sultanahmet

HANEDAN

www.hanedanhotel.com

If you want to enjoy Ottoman style on a budget, try this small hotel in the heart of the Sultanahmet hotel district. It has 10 rooms, which are tastefully decorated with pale yellow walls, and its rooftop breakfast terrace gives you fabulous views.

H11 Adliye Sokağı 3, Sultanahmet 212-516-4869 Sultanahmet

ORIENT HOSTEL

www.orienthostel.com

This hostel, with 92 beds in single and twin rooms and dorms, is at the heart of the backpacker scene, with hookah and occasional movie nights, a travel agency and free internet access for guests. It also has a terrace café and restaurant.

H11 Akbıyık Caddesi 13, Sultanahmet 212-517-9493 Sultanahmet

PENINSULA

www.hotelpeninsula.com

On the same quiet street as the Hanedan (▷ this page), this small hotel in a restored cream-painted town house, has 11 rooms and a penthouse suite, plus a roof terrace where you can lie on a hammock and relax, enjoying the dreamy views of the Blue Mosque and the Sea of Marmara.

H11 Adliye Sokağı 6, Sultanahmet 212-458-6850 Sultanahmet

ROOM WITH A VIEW

If you're on a budget and can't afford to stay in a first-class hotel, you should still be able to find a 'room with a view' in Istanbul. Most of the lower-price hotels in Sultanahmet have a rooftop breakfast terrace or bar where you relax afer a day of sightseeing or shopping. Other extras that may be included are free internet access and a transfer from the airport—remember to ask about this when you book. You can sometimes get a discount by paying in cash, especially if you pay in euros or US dollars.

SIDE HOTEL AND PENSION

www.sidehotel .com

One of the best options for those on a budget, this large establishment in Sultanahmet has a wide range of accommodation, choose from en suite hotel rooms to pension rooms with shared bathrooms, and family apartments.

G11 Utangaç Sokağı 20, Sultanahmet 212-517-2282 Sultanahmet

SULTAN'S INN

www.sultansinn.com

An Ottoman-style hotel in a convenient location but in the budget category, this pretty mustard-painted town house in the Küçük Ayasofya district has stone walls, warm Anatolian fabrics and the obligatory roof terrace.

F12 Mustafa Paşa Sokağı 50, Sultanahmet 212-638-2562 Sultanahmet

Mid-Range Hotels

PRICES

Expect to pay between €90 and €150 per night for a double room in a mid-range hotel.

AMISOS

www.amisoshotel.com

This boutique hotel opposite Gülhane Park has the feel of an Ottoman harem, with rooms decorated in blue, pink and black or with sumptuous red velvet drapes. By contrast, the North Shield British-style pub is on the ground floor.

G9 Ebusuud Caddesi 2, Gülhane 212-512-7050 Gülhane

ARARAT

www.ararathotel.com

Small (12 rooms), arty hotel with dark wooden floors, canopy beds and Byzantine-inspired murals. The rooftop bar has lovely views over the Sea of Marmara.

G11 Torun Sokağı 3, Sultanahmet 212-516-0411 Sultanahmet

ARTEFES

www.artefes.com

This striking Ottoman wooden house, with flower-filled window boxes, is hidden away in the backstreets of Küçük Ayasofya. On warm days, enjoy breakfast on the rooftop terrace.

F12 Çayiroğlu Sokağı 25, Sultanahmet 212-516-5863 Sultanahmet

ASMALI KONAK

www.asmalikonakhotel.com

Opened in 2007 in a family-owned town house in Küçük Ayasofya, the 'house of the vine' has 16 rooms, decorated in classical Turkish style with antiques.

F12 Mustafa Paşa Sokağı 57, Sultanahmet 212-638-3534 Sultanahmet

AYASOFYA KONAKLARI

www.ayasofyakonaklari.com

Istanbul's original Ottoman-style hotel consists of 64 rooms in a row of beautifully converted wooden houses in pastel shades and decorated in period style. The hotel takes up a cobbled street between Ayasofya and Topkapı Palace.

H10 Soğukçeşme Sokağı, Sultanahmet 212-513-3660 Gülhane

OTTOMAN CHIC

The first Ottoman-style hotels appeared in Istanbul in the 1980s, when the Turkish Touring and Automobile Club renovated a number of buildings of historical and architectural importance, such as the Ayasofya Konaklari (▷ this page). Now there are numerous private hotels in the Sultanahmet district, many in the brightly painted wooden houses that are typical of the area. They all offer variations on Ottoman chic, which combines traditional fabrics and furniture with modern comforts and design, which makes them great places to stay.

DERSAADET

www.hoteldersaadet.com

Dersaadet is a restored 19th-century wooden mansion with 17 rooms, with old-style wooden furniture and parquet floors, and a breakfast terrace with views of the Blue Mosque.

G12 Kapı Agasi Sokağı 5, Küçük Ayasofya, Sultanahmet 212-458-0760 Sultanahmet

EMPRESS ZOE

www.emzoe.com

Named after a legendary 11th-century Byzantine empress, this tastefully converted stone house is the classic Ottoman-style hotel, with stone walls, wooden floors, a wrought-iron staircase (no lift), kilims and textiles and a 15th-century hammam in the garden. There are 22 rooms.

H11 Adliye Sokağı, Akbıyık Caddesi 4/1, Sultanahmet 212-518-2504 Sultanahmet

ERESIN CROWN

www.eresin.com.tr/eresincrown

The only five-star hotel in

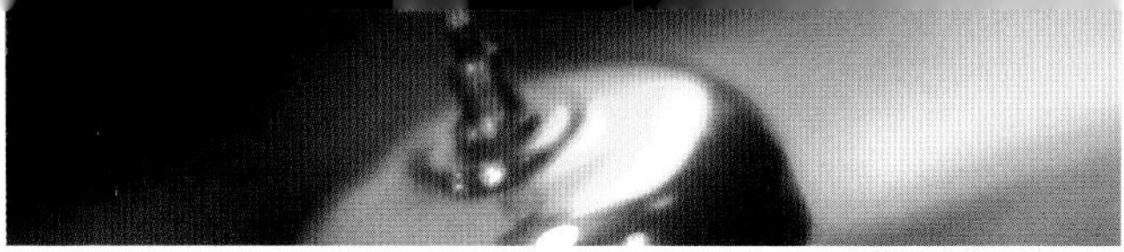

Küçük Ayasofya has a rooftop restaurant and an archaeological museum displaying Roman and Byzantine remains discovered during its construction.
F12 Küçük Ayasofya Caddesi 40, Sultanahmet
212-638-4428
Sultanahmet

IBRAHIM PAŞHA

www.ibrahimpasha.com

This small boutique hotel with 24 rooms, in a stone townhouse, combines Ottoman features with modern designer touches, such as flat-screen TVs and wireless internet access. There's also a roof terrace with good views.
F11 Terzihane Sokağı 7, Sultanahmet 212-518-0394 Sultanahmet

KARIYE

www.kariyeotel.com

Kariye is a tastefully converted Ottoman wooden house with Turkish carpets, parquet floor and prints of old Istanbul in its 26 rooms, as well as the excellent Asitane restaurant (▷ 74).
b5 Kariye Camii Sokağı 6, Edirnekapı 212-534-8414 Edirnekapı

KYBELE

www.kybelehotel.com

This small hotel near the Hippodrome is quirky and bright, with antique lanterns hanging from every ceiling and rooms that are filled with kilims and knick-knacks.
G10 Yerebatan Caddesi 35, Sultanahmet
212-511-7766
Sultanahmet

NOMADE

www.hotelnomade.com

In a busy restaurant area at the foot of Divan Yolu (▷ 38), this trendy hotel, run by two sisters, has 16 rooms that are painted in bright modern hues, as well as a lovely roof terrace.
G10 Ticarethane Sokağı 15, Sultanahmet
212-513-8172
Sultanahmet

NORTH OF THE GOLDEN HORN

If you want to stay in Beyoğlu, close to the shopping, restaurants and nightlife, there are two good hotels in restored 19th-century buildings. The Richmond Hotel (212-252-5460; www.richmondhotels.com.tr) is the only hotel on Istiklâl Caddesi (▷ 80–81), while the Anemon Galata (212-293-2343; www.anemonhotels.com) is on Galata Square, near the Galata Tower (▷ 82–83). Both have rooftop bars with stunning views. Rooms at both hotels start at around €100–€130 per night.

POEM

www.hotelpoem.com

A 19th-century Ottoman wooden mansion, Poem has been converted into a tasteful small hotel, with 17 rooms named after Turkish poems. There is a roof garden and also a breakfast terrace shaded by walnut and fig trees.
H11 Terbıyık Sokağı 12, Sultanahmet
212-638-9744
Sultanahmet

SARNIÇ

www.sarnichotel.com

This elegant hotel, completely renovated in 2010, is named after the magnificent fifth-century Byzantine cistern in the basement. The hotel has 16 rooms and a rooftop restaurant with views of the Blue Mosque. Guests can take a four-hour Ottoman cookery class with the resident chef.
G12 Küçük Ayasofya Caddesi 26, Sultanahmet
212-518-2323
Sultanahmet

SOKULLU PAŞA

www.sokullupasahotel.com

Sokullu Paşa, in a 16th-century pink clapboard house, has 37 rooms, decorated in traditional style, and excellent facilities, including a hammam and delightful garden.
F11 Şehit Mehmet Paşa Sokağı 5, Sultanahmet
212-518-1790
Sultanahmet

Luxury Hotels

PRICES

Expect to pay more than €150 per night for a double room in a luxury hotel.

BENTLEY

www.bentley-hotel.com

With its minimalist decor and achingly hip design, the Bentley was Istanbul's first boutique hotel—just the place to stay for a shopping spree in the nearby fashion stores of Teşvikiye and Nişantaşı.

Off map at J1 Halaskargazi Caddesi 75, Harbiye 212-291-7730 Harbiye

ÇIRAĞAN PALACE KEMPINSKI

www.ciraganpalace.com

This 19th-century sultan's palace is now a five-star hotel with magnificent views across the Bosphorus and every conceivable luxury. Many of its 315 rooms and suites have sea views and most are in a modern annex.

Off map at J4 Çırağan Caddesi 32, Beşiktaş 212-258-3377 Beşiktaş

FOUR SEASONS

www.fourseasons.com/istanbul

In a former high-security prison in Sultanahmet, the Four Seasons is now the best address in town, with an open courtyard and 65 luxury rooms in the old cells.

H11 Tevkifhane Sokağı 1, Sultanahmet 212-402-3000 Sultanahmet

MARMARA TAKSIM

www.themarmarahotels.com

This huge skyscraper on Taksim Square, located close to the shops, restaurants and nightlife of Beyoğlu. The 468 rooms are well appointed and have fine views of the Bosphorus and the Sea of Marmara from the rooftop bar.

J2 Taksim Meydanı 212-251-4696 Taksim Taksim

PERA PALACE

Istanbul's most celebrated hotel (▷ 83) opened for business in 1895 for passengers arriving in Constantinople after their 68-hour journey on the Orient Express train from Paris. The last word in luxury, the hotel acquired its aura of mystery and suspense after crime writer Agatha Christie stayed here while writing her novel *Murder on the Orient Express*. Other famous guests have included the spy Mata Hari, film star Greta Garbo and Turkish president Kemal Atatürk. The Pera Palace reopened for business in September 2010 after an extensive restoration but has lost none of its period glamour, and a superb place to stay in Instanbul.

LES OTTOMANS

www.lesottomans.com

With suites starting at just over €1,000 per night, including butler service, fitness center and vinotherapy spa, this hotel is the ultimate in decadence and chic. It opened in 2006 in a wooden mansion beside the Bosphorus.

Off map at J4 Muallim Naci Caddesi 68, Kuruçeşme 212-359-1500 Ortaköy

TURQUHOUSE

www.turquhouse.com

Experience views of the Golden Horn like those enjoyed by French traveler Pierre Loti at this Ottoman-style boutique hotel near the famous café (▷ 66). There are 67 rooms with satellite TV, and amenities include sauna, Turkish bath, free WiFi and a choice of places to eat.

Off map at B1 Merkez Mahallesi, Idris Köşkü Caddesi, Eyüp 212-497-1313 Eyüp, then taxi

YEŞIL EV

www.istanbulyesilev.com

The 'green house' is a restored 19th-century Ottoman wooden mansion between Ayasofya and the Blue Mosque, with 19 rooms decorated in period style and a beautiful garden with a fountain at the heart.

G11 Kabasakal Caddesi 5, Sultanahmet 212-517-6785 Sultanahmet

Need to Know

This section gives you all the practical information you need to plan your visit and make the most of your time in Istanbul.

Planning Ahead

When to Go

Istanbul is busiest from May to September, when the weather is consistently warm and sunny. In July and August the city can become uncomfortably hot and crowded and many locals escape to the islands or coast. The most pleasant times to visit are in late spring and early autumn.

TIME

Istanbul is two hours ahead of London, seven hours ahead of New York and ten hours ahead of Los Angeles.

AVERAGE DAILY MAXIMUM TEMPERATURES

JAN	FEB	MAR	APR	MAY	JUN	JUL	AUG	SEP	OCT	NOV	DEC
47°F	48°F	52°F	62°F	70°F	79°F	82°F	82°F	77°F	67°F	59°F	52°F
8°C	9°C	11°C	17°C	21°C	26°C	28°C	28°C	25°C	19°C	15°C	11°C

Winter (Dec–Feb) is cold, wet and windy with gray skies. There is frequent rain and occasional sleet and snow.

Spring (Mar–May) is a delightful time, with mild weather, longer days and the start of the tourist season.

Summer (Jun–Aug) is hot and humid, though evenings by the Bosphorus can be pleasantly cool. There are also occasional thunderstorms.

Autumn (Sep–Nov) brings rain, though the sea is still warm enough for swimming in September.

WHAT'S ON

April *International Film Festival:* New releases of Turkish and foreign films are shown.

National Sovereignty and Children's Day (23 April): School children parade along Istiklâl Caddesi.

May *International Theater Festival:* This drama event is held in even-numbered years.

Fatih Day (29 May): Marching bands, parades and fireworks mark the Ottoman conquest of Constantinople by Mehmet the Conqueror in 1453.

June/July *International Music Festival:* Istanbul's biggest cultural event sees concerts and recitals at venues including Aya Irini church (▷ 38).

July *International Jazz Festival:* An offshoot of the International Music Festival (▷ above).

July/August *Starry Nights:* Open-air rock, pop and folk concerts are held in the magnificent setting of the Ottoman fortress at Rumeli Hisarı (▷ 101) and in the open-air arena at Harbiye.

September/October *Akbank Jazz Festival:* Traditional and modern jazz concerts are held at venues throughout the city.

Republic Day (29 October): Patriotic displays and fireworks mark the anniversary of the proclamation of the Turkish Republic in 1923.

November *Anniversary of Atatürk's Death* (10 November): One minute's silence is observed across the city at 9.05am, the exact time of Kemal Atatürk's death.

Useful Websites

www.istanbul.gov.tr
The official site of the Istanbul Governor's office features history, tourist sights, a photo gallery and a weather forecast.

www.ibb.gov.tr
The Istanbul Metropolitan Municipality site has maps, photos and practical advice.

www.gototurkey.co.uk/
www.tourismturkey.co.uk
Official sites of the Turkish Tourist Office in the UK and US, with practical information.

www.kultur.gov.tr
Website of the Ministry of Culture and Tourism, with good background information on Turkish arts, crafts and traditions.

www.mymerhaba.com
This expat's website includes Istanbul city life, culture, entertainment, events, listings.

www.turkeytravelplanner.com
Personal site of writer and Turkey expert Tim Brosnahan, packed with travel advice and amusing anecdotes and tips.

www.timeoutistanbul.com
Online version of the monthly *Time Out* magazine, with the lowdown on the hottest restaurants, clubs and bars, as well as up-to-date listings of films, music and sports.

www.millisaraylar.gov.tr
Official site of the national palaces, including Dolmabahçe, Beylerbeyi and Yıldız Şale.

www.hurriyetdailynews.com
Turkey's English-language newspaper.

www.kapalicarsi.org.tr
Listings for every shop in the Grand Bazaar.

GOOD TRAVEL SITES

www.fodors.com
A complete travel-planning site. Book air tickets, cars and rooms, research prices and weather, pose questions to fellow tourists, and find links to other sites.

www.thy.com
Turkish Airlines site, with online booking facility.

www.ido.com.tr
Schedules, fares and passenger information for ferry and seabus services.

INTERNET CAFÉS

Adeks
Barberos Bulvar 59a
212-227-5778
Daily 7am–2am
2 TL per hour

Legend
Peykhane Caddesi 16
212-518-3348
Daily 9am–midnight
2 TL per hour

Otantik
Alayköškü Caddesi 2
212-511-2433
Daily 9am–midnight
3 TL per hour

Yuva
Yeni Carši Caddesi 8/4
212-244-8959
Daily 9am–midnight
3 TL per hour

Getting There

INSURANCE

As Turkey does not have reciprocal health-care agreements with other countries it is essential that all visitors take out comprehensive medical and emergency insurance.

GETTING YOUR BEARINGS

Istanbul can be a bit disorientating for first-time visitors, but really it is very simple to navigate. The main sights are concentrated in Sultanahmet, south of the Golden Horn on the European side and connected to Atatürk airport by the coast road along the Sea of Marmara. North of the Golden Horn but still in Europe, Beyoğlu is the shopping, entertainment and nightlife quarter. The Bosphorus strait, which links the Sea of Marmara to the Black Sea, separates European from Asian Turkey and effectively divides the city in two.

AIRPORTS

Istanbul's main airport, Atatürk International Airport (IST), is 13.5km (8 miles) west of the city and has regular flights to major European, American and Asian cities. Facilities for visitors include car rental, exchange bureaux, ATMs, post office, pharmacy and tourist information office.

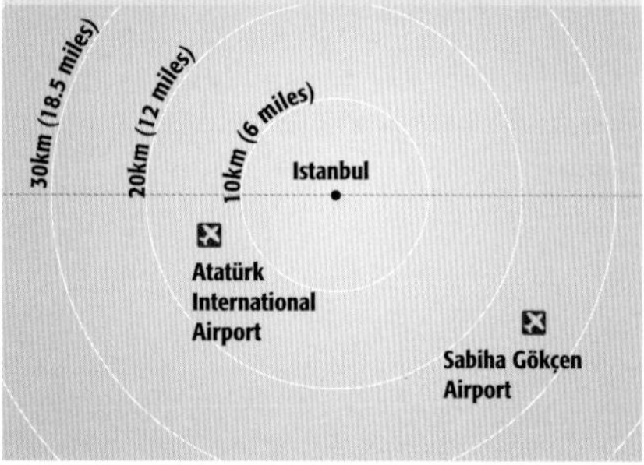

ARRIVING AT ATATÜRK INTERNATIONAL AIRPORT

The primary international airport is Atatürk International Airport (IST), ☎ 212-465-5555. Some hotels provide free taxi or minibus shuttle services if you are staying more than three nights, so ask about this when you book. Otherwise the most convenient way of reaching the city by public transport is on the Metro/Light Rail Transit in the direction of Aksaray. Change at Zeytinburnu station for the tram to Sultanahmet or Eminönü. The Metro station is on the lower ground floor of the airport. Both Metro and tram run every 10 minutes or so from 6am

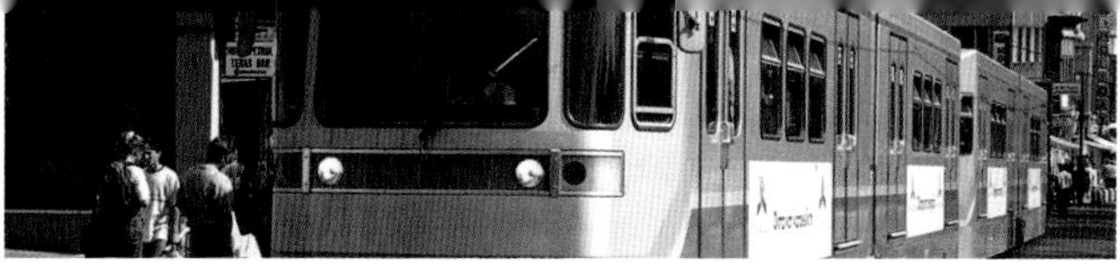

to midnight and a *jeton* (token) for each section of the journey costs around 1.50 TL.

If you are staying north of the Golden Horn, the Havaš airport bus (www.havas.net) leaves every 30 minutes, from 5am to midnight, and costs 10 TL for the 1-hour journey to Taksim Square.

A taxi from the airport to Sultanahmet or Beyoğlu will cost around €20 or 40 TL.

ARRIVING AT SABIHA GÖKÇEN AIRPORT
Istanbul's second airport is around 26km (16 miles) east of Kadıköy on the Asian shore of the Bosphorus at Kurtköy (☎ 216-588-8000). It mostly handles domestic and budget flights, including those operated by EasyJet from London Luton. To reach the heart of the city by public transport, take bus number E10, which has regular departures from the airport. It takes about an hour to reach Kadıköy, where you can catch a ferry to Eminönü. Havaş airport buses leave shortly after the arrival of incoming flights and cost 10 TL to Kadıköy and 13 TL to Taksim Square via the Bosphorus Bridge. A taxi to Sultanahmet or Beyoğlu will cost around €30 or 100 TL.

ARRIVING BY BUS
Long-distance and international buses arrive at the Otogar (bus station), 10km (6 miles) west of the city. Some bus companies offer a free minibus transfer into the city. The Metro from Atatürk airport to Aksaray stops at the Otogar; change at Aksaray for a tram to Sultanahmet or Eminönü. Buses from Asian Turkey arrive at Harem, from where you can catch a ferry to Eminönü.

ARRIVING BY TRAIN
Trains from European destinations arrive at Sirkeci station (☎ 212-522-2280), with onward connections by bus, tram and ferry. Trains from Asian destinations arrive at Haydarpaşa station (☎ 212-336-0475), near Kadıköy, from where you can pick up a ferry to Eminönü.

ENTRY REQUIREMENTS

Citizens of the UK, US, Canada, Australia and some EU countries need a visa, which can be purchased online before you travel, and is valid for multiple entries to Turkey over a three-month period. To check if you require a visa, and purchase one if necessary, visit www.evisa.gov.tr. Expect to pay approximately $20. Citizens of New Zealand and some EU countries, including France, Germany and Greece, just require a valid passport. Regulations can change, so always check before you travel.

CUSTOMS

- Duty-free allowances: 200 cigarettes, 50 cigars, 200g tobacco, 1 liter of wine and spirits. Additional allowance: 400 cigarettes, 100 cigars, 500g tobacco if you buy from a Turkish duty-free shop on arrival.
- Valuables should be registered on your passport on entry.
- Keep proofs of purchase for expensive items.
- The export of antiquities is forbidden.

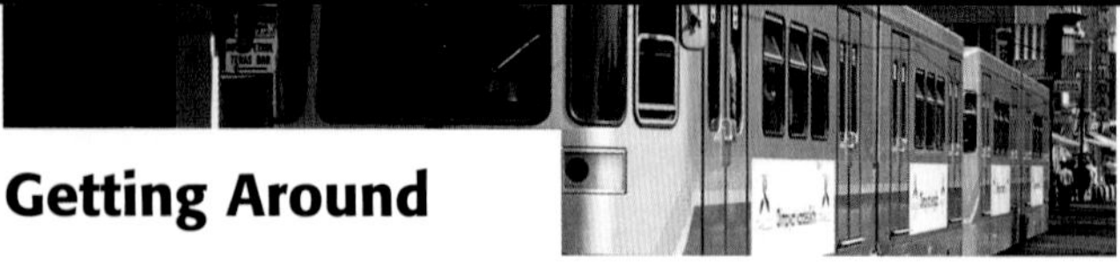

Getting Around

AKBIL TAG & ISTANBULKART

One feature of the system that is useful for visitors is the Akbil tag, an electronic 'smart button' attached to a plastic holder, which contains credit for journeys. Akbil tags can be bought for a refundable deposit of 10 TL at major bus and Metro terminals, including Aksaray, Eminönü, Sirkeci and Zeytinburnu. They can be charged with any amount of credit and used to pay for journeys by pressing the button into the electronic machine at turnstiles and on buses. Akbil fares are around 10 per cent lower than regular fares, so you save money as well as time queueing for tickets. Akbil tags are valid on buses, trams, the Metro, suburban trains, ferries, seabuses, the Tünel and Taksim funiculars, the Istiklâl Caddesi tramway and the cable car from Eyüp to the Pierre Loti Café (▷ panel, 66). The Akbil Tag is gradually being phased out in favor of the new Istanbulkart: prepaid rechargeable travel cards, sold at Istanbulkart vending machines. Cards cost 10 TL and can be topped up with a credit card, as required. Eventually, the Istanbulkart will be used for taxis, museums, movie theaters and theaters.

Istanbul has a comprehensive and well integrated public transport network, including buses, trams, local trains, the Metro, funicular and ferries.

BUSES, TRAMS, TRAINS AND FUNICULAR

- The bus network is extensive, but travel is slow and vehicles are often crowded. Maps are displayed at bus stops and at major bus stations such as Eminönü and Taksim. The destination is shown on the front of the bus.
- Tickets can be bought at bus terminals and kiosks that display the sign '*IETT otobüs bileti*'. Drop the ticket into the box near the driver.
- The main tram route begins at Zeytinburnu and passes through Aksaray, Beyazıt, Çemberlitaş, Gülhane, Sirkeci and Eminönü before crossing the Galata Bridge to Karaköy and continuing via Tophane to Kabataş. Trams run every few minutes from 6am to midnight. *Jetons* are sold at kiosks beside the tram stops and must be fed into the turnstiles to enter the platform.
- Suburban trains from Sirkeci station follow the Marmara shore to Kumkapı, Yenikapı and Yedikule.
- The Tünel funicular railway, opened in 1875, connects the Karaköy end of Galata Bridge with Tünel Square, at the southern end of Istiklâl Caddesi. Trains run every few minutes from 7am to 10pm.
- A modern funicular, opened in 2006, links the end of the tram line at Kabataş with the Metro station beneath Taksim Square.
- A vintage tram service runs along Istiklâl Caddesi, linking Tünel with Taksim Square, useful after a day on your feet.

DOLMUŞES AND TAXIS

- The most common form of transport in Istanbul is the ubiquitous yellow taxi. Although taxis are more expensive than other means of public transport, they are still relatively inexpensive and are a convenient way to get

around. All fares are metered. Higher rates apply after midnight.

- *Dolmuşes* (shared taxis) are even cheaper. They follow assigned routes and stop on demand. Destinations are indicated on the windscreen (windshield). You are charged for the distance covered.

FERRIES

- Ferries ply up and down the Bosphorus and the Golden Horn.
- Timetables are posted outside the waiting room at ferry docks.
- Buy a *jeton* from the ticket window and drop it into the turnstile to enter the waiting area.
- When the boat is ready to leave, the doors will open for you to board. The main departure point is Eminönü, where jetties (*iskele*) serve the Golden Horn, Bosphorus (round-trip), Üsküdar, Kadıköy and Harem (car ferry). Ferries to the Princes' Islands depart from Kabataş. For timetables and routes, pick up a leaflet at Eminönü dock or call Ido (☎ 212-444-4436; www.ido.com.tr).
- Fast catamarans or seabuses (*deniz otobüsü*) ply busy commuter routes from Yenikapı and Kabataş.

METRO

- A short Metro commuter line heads north from Taksim to Levent, convenient for the Akmerkez and Metro City shopping malls.
- A second Metro commuter line connects Atatürk International Airport to Aksaray, 3km (2 miles) west of Sultanahmet. One of the stops is at the *Otogar* (bus station). The stations at Aksaray and Zeytinburnu are convenient interchanges for the tram line to Sultanahmet and Eminönü.
- Construction work is under way to extend both Metro lines to the seabus terminal at Yenikapı, linking them with each other.
- *Jetons* for the Metro are sold at stations and must be fed into the turnstiles to enter the platform.

PLANNING AHEAD

Istanbul's public transport infrastructure was struggling to cope with the growing population, and its popularity as a tourist destination so in the last few years major investment has been taking place, which should be complete by 2014. The Marmaray Project, begun in 2004, will create an uninterrupted 76km (48-mile) rail link from Halkali on the European side to Gebze in Asia. The highlight, completed in 2010, is a tunnel beneath the Bosphorus from Sirkeci to Üsküdar. Construction work of the tunnel unearthed Byzantine relics, which are now on display in the Archaeological Museum (▷ 24).

VISITORS WITH DISABILITIES

Istanbul is not an easy city for visitors with disabilities to negotiate. Streets are crowded and uneven, and few public buildings, toilets or transport facilities are wheelchair-accessible. There are plans to improve access to buses, trams and ferries, but for the time being provision for visitors with disabilities is limited. Both the Blue Mosque and Hagia Sophia are moderately accessible for wheelchair-users.

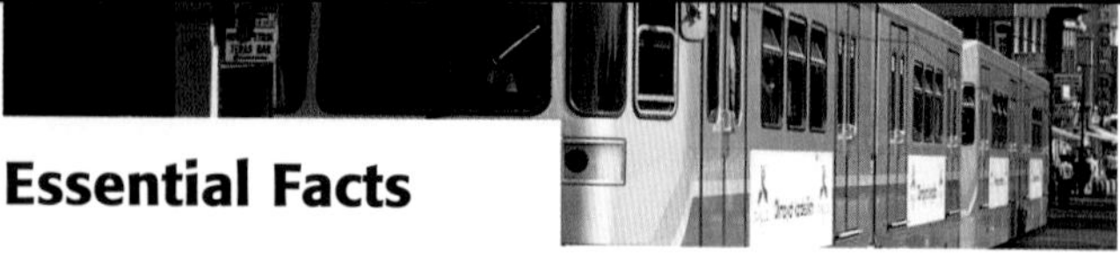

Essential Facts

CONSULATES

- **Australia** ✉ Asker Ocaği Caddesi 15, Elmadağ ☎ 212-243-1333; www.turkey.embassy.gov.au
- **Canada** ✉ Istiklâl Caddesi 189/5, Beyoğlu ☎ 212-251-9838; www.canadainternational.gc.ca/turkey
- **Ireland** ✉ Ali Riza Gürcan Caddesi, Merter ☎ 212-482-2434; www.dfa.ie/home
- **UK** BMeşrutiyet Caddesi 34, Tepebaşı ☎ 212-334-6400; www.ukinturkey.fco.gov.uk
- **US** ✉ Kaplıcalar Mevkii 2, Istinye ☎ 212-335-9000; www.istanbul.usconsulate.gov

EMERGENCY PHONE NUMBERS

- Fire ☎ 110
- Ambulance ☎ 112
- Police ☎ 155
- Tourist Police ☎ 212-527-4503

ELECTRICITY

- 220 volts AC; two-pronged round-pin plugs are used.

ETIQUETTE

- Turkish people are generally friendly, polite and modest—you will earn their respect if you behave in the same way.
- When visiting mosques wear longer skirts or trousers and long-sleeved tops. Women should cover their heads.
- Always remove your shoes when you enter a mosque and a Turkish house or apartment.

MEDICAL TREATMENT

- There is no free health care for visitors, so make sure you have health insurance.
- For minor ailments, go to a pharmacy.
- Private hospitals: American Hospital; www.americanhospitalistanbul.org ✉ Güzelbahçe Sokak, Nişantaşı ☎ 212-444-3777; Florence Nightingale Hospital ✉ Abidei Hürriyet Caddesi 290, Çağlayan Şişli ☎ 212-375-6161; International Hospital BIstanbul Caddesi 82, Yeşilköy ☎ 212-468-4444
- State hospital: Taksim Ilk Yardim Hastanesi (for emergency treatment only) ✉ Siraselviler Caddesi 112, Beyoğlu ☎ 212-252-4300

MEDICINES

- Pharmacies sell imported drugs as well as local medicines.
- Pharmacists are qualified to take your blood pressure and administer first aid.
- Pharmacists have a 24-hour rota service: addresses are displayed in their windows.

OPENING HOURS

- Shops: Mon–Sat 9–7; malls daily 10–10
- Government offices: Mon–Fri 9–12.30, 1.30–5
- Banks: Mon–Fri 9–12, 1.30–5
- All are closed on public holidays and the first day(s) of religious holidays.

PLACES OF WORSHIP

- Mosques: There are more than 2,500 mosques in Istanbul.
- Greek Orthodox Patriarchate: ✉ Sadrazam Ali Paşa Caddesi, Fener ☎ 212-531-9670
- Roman Catholic: St. Antony BIstiklâl Caddesi 325, Beyoğlu ☎ 212-244-0935
- Protestant: German Church ✉ Emin Camii Sokağı 40, Beyoğlu ☎ 212-250-3040
- Anglican: Christ Church ✉ Serdarı Ekrem Sokağı 82 ☎ 212-251-5616
- Synagogues: Neve Shalom ✉ Büyük Hendek Caddesi 61, Şişhane ☎ 212-293-7566; Askhenazi BBanker Sokak 10, Yüksekkaldırım Caddesi, Karaköy ☎ 212-243-6909

POSTAL SERVICE

- Stamps are sold from post offices and some shops selling postcards.
- Post boxes are yellow, but you may find it more reliable to drop your letters off at a post office.
- PTT (Post-Telephone-Telegram) signs are written in black on a yellow background.
- The main post office (open daily) is at Şehin Şah Pehlevi Caddesi, near Sirkeci station. Other post offices are in Galatasaray Meydanı in Beyoğlu and the Grand Bazaar.

SENSIBLE PRECAUTIONS

- Take sunglasses, a hat and sun-screen.
- Avoid raw foods and ice cubes.
- Tap water is officially safe to drink but it is heavily chlorinated. Bottled water is widely available.
- Watch your valuables in crowded locations and don't leave them in hotel rooms.
- Mugging, bag-snatching and other street crimes are not common in Istanbul, but avoid isolated areas at night.
- Do not get into a taxi that already has a passenger.
- Act with the same caution as in other cities.

LOST PROPERTY

Report lost passports to the Tourist Police ✉ Yerebatan Caddesi, Sultanahmet ☎ 212-527-4503

MONEY

The official currency is the Turkish Lira (TL). Old YTL banknotes, introduced in 2005, were withdrawn from circulation at the end of 2009 but can be exchanged for Turkish lira notes at branches of the Central Bank of Turkey until 1 January 2020. Notes are in denominations of 5, 10, 20, 50, 100 and a new 200 lira note.

NATIONAL HOLIDAYS

- 1 Jan: New Year's Day
- 23 Apr: National Sovereignty and Children's Day
- 1 May: May Day (Istanbul only)
- 19 May: Youth and Sports Day
- 30 Aug: Victory Day
- 29 Oct: Republic Day

In addition to these, the major Islamic religious holidays (▷ below) are also national holidays.

RELIGIOUS HOLIDAYS

- The holy month of Ramadan, when Muslims fast between sunrise and sunset, lasts for four weeks before Şeker Bayramı.
- Şeker Bayramı (three days, dates vary).
- Kurban Bayramı (four days, dates vary).

TIPPING

It is usual to leave about 10 percent of the bill as a tip (gratuity) in restaurants. Like everywhere else, taxi drivers appreciate a small tip, and you are also expected to tip masseurs and attendants at hammams (Turkish baths).

TELEPHONES

- Public telephone booths use a phonecard, which can be bought at post offices and kiosks in amounts of 50, 100 and 200 units.
- The code for Istanbul is 212 on the European side and 216 on the Asian side. To call a number on the same side of the Bosphorus, omit the prefix. For calls across the Bosphorus, dial 0 before the number, including the prefix.
- For international calls, dial 00, followed by the country code (US = 1, UK = 44) before the number.
- To call Istanbul from abroad, dial the international access code (US = 011, UK = 00), followed by 90, then the full number.
- International operator ☎ 115
- Directory assistance ☎ 118
- Most mobile phones will connect to local networks if you have arranged international roaming. Mobile numbers start with 05.

TOILETS

- There are toilets near mosques and in museums and cafés. It is customary to leave a small tip in the plate by the door.
- A few old-style toilets (two footholds and a hole in the ground) still exist in Istanbul.

TOURIST OFFICES

- Official guides can be booked through tourist information offices (▷ below).
- There are also plenty of unofficial guides willing to help. Agree on a price before you embark on a trip.
- The most useful office is in Sultanahmet, at the northeastern end of the Hippodrome ☎ 212-518-1802 🕒 Daily 9–5.
- There is a 24-hour tourist office in the arrivals hall at Atatürk International Airport, and tourist information counters for arriving passengers at Sirkeci station and Karaköy shipping terminal. There is also a tourist information office on Cumhuriyet Caddesi, in the arcade in front of the Istanbul Hilton.

Language

USEFUL PHRASES	
hello	*merhaba*
goodbye	*allaha ısmarladık (person going)*
goodbye	*güle güle (person staying)*
yes	*evet*
no	*hayır/yok*
please	*lütfen*
thank you	*teşekkür ederim/mersi*
you're welcome	*bir şey değil*
I don't understand	*sizi anlamiyorum*
do you speak English?	*Ingilizce biliyor musunuz?*
open	*açik*
closed	*kapalı*
leave me alone	*bırak beni*

HOTELS	
hotel	*hotel/otel*
bed-and-breakfast	*pansiyon*
do you have a room?	*boş odanız var mi?*
single/double/triple	*tek/çift/üç kişilik*
I have a reservation	*reservasyonım var*
balcony	*balkon*
elevator	*asansör*
room service	*oda servisi*
air-conditioning	*klima*
hot water	*sicak su*
bath	*banyo*

RESTAURANTS	
I'd like a table for two	*Iki kişilik bir masa*
menu	*fiyat listesi*
soup	*çorba*
fish	*balık*
meat/vegetarian dishes	*etli/etsiz yemekler*
red/white wine	*kırmızı/beyaz şarap*
bill	*hesap*
service included	*servos dahilli*

TRANSPORT	
aeroplane	*uçak*
airport	*havaalanı*
train	*tren*
railway station	*tren ıstasyonu*
bus	*otobus*
bus stop	*emanet*
bus station	*otogar*
taxi	*taksi*
car	*araba*
petrol	*benzin*
boat	*gemi*
ferry	*vapur/feribot*
port	*liman*
ticket	*bilet*
single/return	*gidiş/gidiş dönüş*

MONEY	
bank	*banka*
exchange office	*döriz*
post office	*postane*
traveler's check	*seyahat çeki*
credit card	*kredi kartı*
exchange rate	*dövis kuru*
how much?	*ne kadar?*
expensive	*pahalı*
what is the price?	*fıatı nedir?*
10	*on*
50	*elli*
100	*yüz*
200	*ikiyüz*
1,000	*bin*

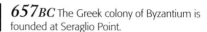

Timeline

SÜLEYMAN THE MAGNIFICENT

The Ottoman empire reached its zenith under Süleyman I, whose 46-year reign, which began in 1520, made him the longest serving of all the sultans. Under his rule, Istanbul became the most powerful city in the world, with territories stretching from Cairo to Budapest. Süleyman fell in love with and married Roxelana, a beautiful Russian slave girl, refusing to take any other wives or concubines. The two of them are buried in the grounds of the Süleymaniye Mosque, the masterpiece of Süleyman's chief architect Mimar Sinan (▷ 54).

657BC The Greek colony of Byzantium is founded at Seraglio Point.

133BC Byzantium becomes part of the Roman province of Asia Minor.

AD330 Emperor Constantine decrees that Byzantium is to be the new capital of the Roman empire.

395 The Roman empire is officially divided into two, with Byzantium (now Constantinople) the capital of the Eastern Roman empire.

412–22 Theodosius II orders the building of a new wall around the city.

527–65 Reign of Emperor Justinian. Ayasofya is built and the empire extends its influence from Spain to Iran.

1204 Constantinople is sacked.

1453 The city falls to Ottoman Sultan Mehmet II after a seven-week siege.

1461–65 The Topkapı Palace is built.

1520–66 Reign of Sultan Süleyman the Magnificent (▷ panel).

1617 Building of the Blue Mosque.

1856 Sultan Abdülmecit moves out of Topkapı Palace and into Dolmabahçe.

Left to right: Atatürk; the siege of Constantinople; Topkapı Palace; the Sultanahmet Camii, also known as the Blue Mosque; the Turkish flag

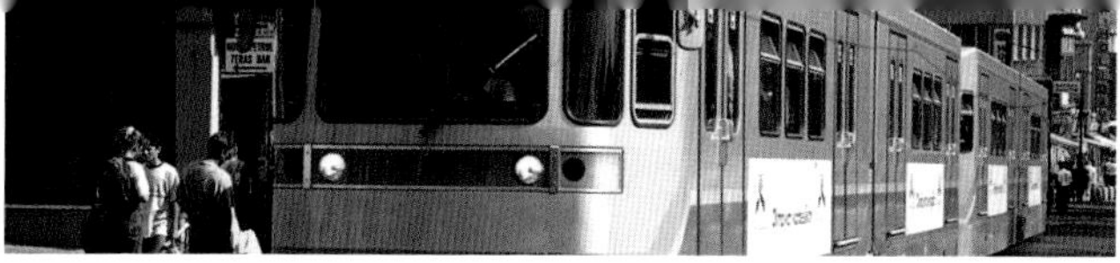

1883 The Orient Express arrives in Istanbul.

1914 Following the Balkan Wars and the collapse of the Ottoman empire, Turkey enters World War I on Germany's side. Allied forces occupy Istanbul at the end of the war.

1922–23 After a three-year War of Independence, Mustafa Kemal Atatürk (▷ panel) proclaims the Turkish Republic, moving the capital from Istanbul to Ankara.

1938 Atatürk dies in Dolmabahçe Palace.

1939–45 Turkey remains neutral during World War II.

1994 Recep Erdoğan of the Islamic Welfare Party is elected mayor of Istanbul.

2003 Over 50 people die in attacks on synagogues, the British consulate and HSBC bank.

2005 Istanbul hosts the Champions League soccer final and the first Turkish Grand Prix. Begins entry talks with the European Union.

2010 Istanbul is joint European Capital of Culture.

2011 PKK kill 24 Turkish troops near the Iraq border, and relations with Syria turn sour.

2013 Protests across Turkey demand freedom of the press, assembly and expression.

KEMAL ATATÜRK

Born in Salonika (Thessaloniki) in 1880, Mustafa Kemal became a national hero after defeating the Allied forces at Gallipoli in 1915. Following the collapse of the Ottoman empire and defeat in World War I, he led a war of independence, expelling all occupying forces from Turkey. As president of the Turkish Republic from 1923 until his death in 1938, he transformed the country, moving the capital to Ankara, abolishing the fez and other forms of religious dress, giving women the vote and introducing the Western calendar and Latin script in an effort to create a secular, European society. In 1934 he adopted the surname Atatürk ('Father of the Turks'), and he is still revered throughout the country as the founding father of the nation.

THE FLAG OF THE REPUBLIC OF TURKEY

Index

INDEX

Istanbul 25 Best

WRITTEN BY Christopher and Melanie Rice
ADDITIONAL WRITING Tony Kelly
UPDATED BY Richard Waters
SERIES EDITOR Clare Ashton
COVER DESIGN Chie Ushio, Yuko Inagaki
DESIGN WORK Tracey Freestone, Nick Johnston
IMAGE RETOUCHING AND REPRO Ian Little

Published in the United Kingdom by AA Publishing

ISBN 978-0-8041-4345-5

THIRD EDITION

SPECIAL SALES
This book is available for special discounts for bulk purchases for sales promotions or premiums. For more information, email specialmarkets@randomhouse.com.

Color separation by AA Digital Department
Printed and bound by Leo Paper Products, China

10 9 8 7 6 5 4 3 2 1

A05141
Mapping in this title produced from mapping © MAIRDUMONT / Falk Verlag 2012
Transport map © Communicarta Ltd, UK

The Automobile Association would like to thank the following photographers, companies and picture libraries for their assistance in the preparation of this book.

Abbreviations for the picture credits are as follows – (t) top; (b) bottom; (c) centre; (l) left; (r) right; (AA) AA World Travel Library.

1 Courtesy of Turkish Culture & Tourist Office; 2 AA/T Souter; 3 AA/T Souter; 4t AA/T Souter; 4b AA/J Pin; 5t AA/T Souter; 5b AA/P Bennett; 6t AA/T Souter; 6cl AA/P Kenward; 6cc AA/D Miterdiri; 6cr AA/C Sawyer; 6bl AA/D Miterdiri; 6bc Courtesy of Turkish Culture & Tourist Office; 6br AA/T Souter; 7t AA/T Souter; 7cl AA/T Souter; 7cc AA/P Kenward; 7cr Courtesy of Turkish Culture & Tourist Office; 7bl Courtesy of Istanbul Modern; 7bc I Keribar/LPI/Getty Images; 7br Dominic Whiting / Alamy; 8t AA/T Souter; 9t AA/T Souter; 10t AA/T Souter; 10/11t AA/J Pin; 10c Courtesy of Turkish Culture & Tourist Office; 11t AA/T Souter; 11c AA/J Pin; 10/11c AA/T Souter; 10/11b AA/C Sawyer; 12t AA/T Souter; 12b Courtesy of Turkish Culture & Tourist Office; 13t AA/T Souter; 13ct AA/P Bennett; 13cb Courtesy of Turkish Culture & Tourist Office; 13b G Yeowell/Image Bank/Getty Images; 14t AA/T Souter; 14ct AA/R Strange; 14cc AA/C Sawyer; 14cb AA/C Sawyer; 14b AA/T Souter; 15t AA/T Souter; 15b Courtesy of Turkish Culture & Tourist Office; 16t AA/T Souter; 16ct Courtesy of Turkish Culture & Tourist Office; 16cc AA/T Souter; 16cb AA/T Souter; 16b Courtesy of Empress Zoe Hotel; 17t AA/T Souter; 17ct Courtesy of Turkish Culture & Tourist Office; 17cc AA/C Sawyer; 17cb Courtesy of Turkish Culture & Tourist Office; 17b Glow Images/ Getty Images; 18t AA/T Souter; 18ct AA/C Sawyer; 18cc AA/A Lawson; 18cb AA/C Sawyer; 18b AA/T Souter; 19t AA/C Sawyer; 19ct AA/P Bennett; 19c AA/C Sawyer; 19cb Courtesy of Turkish Culture & Tourist Office; 19b AA/T Souter; 20/21 AA/C Sawyer; 24l AA/P Bennett; 24r Courtesy of Turkish Culture & Tourist Office; 25l AA/C Sawyer; 25c AA/T Souter; 25r AA/C Sawyer; 26l AA/P Bennett; 26tr AA/T Souter; 26br AA/D Miterdiri; 27t AA/P Kenward; 27bl AA/C Sawyer; 27br AA/T Souter; 28l AA/C Sawyer; 28r IML Image Group Ltd/Alamy; 29l AA/T Souter; 29r AA/T Souter; 30l Courtesy of Turkish Culture & Tourist Office; 30tr AA/T Souter; 30br AA/T Souter; 31t AA/T Souter; 31bl AA/T Souter; 31br AA/C Sawyer; 32l AA/P Bennett; 32tr AA/T Souter; 32br AA/P Bennett; 33t AA/C Sawyer; 33bl AA/C Sawyer; 33br Courtesy of Turkish Culture & Tourist Office; 34l AA/P Bennett; 34tr AA/P Bennett; 34br AA/D Miterdiri; 35t AA/P Bennett; 35bl AA/C Sawyer; 35br AA/T Souter; 36l AA/C Sawyer; 36c AA/T Souter; 36r AA/C Sawyer; 37l AA/C Sawyer; 37r AA/T Souter; 38t Courtesy of Turkish Culture & Tourist Office; 38bl AA/T Souter; 38br AA/P Kenward; 39t Courtesy of Turkish Culture & Tourist Office; 39b AA/D Miterdiri; 40 AA/P Bennett; 41 AA/T Souter; 42 AA/P Kenward; 43 AA/D Miterdiri; 44 AA/T Souter; 45 AA/C Sawyer; 48l AA/P Bennett; 48c AA/C Sawyer; 48r AA/T Souter; 49l Courtesy of Cemberlitas Hamami/Pascal Meunier; 49r AA/P Kenward; 50l AA/P Bennett; 50tr AA/T Souter; 50br AA/T Souter; 51t AA/P Bennett; 51bl AA/P Bennett; 51br AA/T Souter; 52l AA/D Miterdiri; 52c AA/C Sawyer; 52r AA/T Souter; 53l AA/C Sawyer; 53r AA/C Sawyer; 54l AA/P Bennett; 54tr AA/T Souter; 54br AA/T Souter; 55t AA/T Souter; 55bl AA/C Sawyer; 55br AA/T Souter; 56t AA/P Kenward; 56bl AA/T Souter; 56br W Krecichwost/Image Bank/Getty Images; 57t AA/P Kenward; 57bl Images&Stories/Alamy; 57br AA/P Bennett; 58 AA/C Sawyer; 59 AA/T Souter; 60 AA/T Souter; 61 David Noton Photography/ Alamy; 62t AA/T Souter; 62c AA/T Souter; 63 AA/T Souter; 66l AA/C Sawyer; 66tr AA/C Sawyer; 66br AA/T Souter; 67t AA/C Sawyer; 67bl AA/P Kenward; 67br AA/C Sawyer; 68l AA/T Souter; 68tr AA/C Sawyer; 68br AA/P Bennett; 69t AA/C Sawyer; 69bl AA/T Souter; 69br AA/T Souter; 70l AA/T Souter; 70r AA/C Sawyer; 71t AA/C Sawyer; 71bl AA/T Souter; 71br AA/C Sawyer; 72t AA/C Sawyer; 72b Sean Sprague/Alamy; 73 AA/P Bennett; 74 Courtesy of Turkish Culture & Tourist Office; 75 Courtesy of Turkish Culture & Tourist Office; 78tl Courtesy of Istanbul Modern; 78tr Courtesy of Istanbul Modern; 78bl Courtesy of Istanbul Modern; 78br Courtesy of Istanbul Modern; 79t Courtesy of Istanbul Modern; 79bl Courtesy of Istanbul Modern; 79br Courtesy of Istanbul Modern; 80t AA/C Sawyer; 80c Courtesy of Turkish Culture & Tourist Office; 81t G Yeowell/Image Bank/Getty Images; 81c AA/C Sawyer; 82t AA/T Souter; 82b Courtesy of Turkish Culture & Tourist Office; 83t AA/T Souter; 83bl Courtesy of Turkish Culture & Tourist Office; 83br AA/P Bennett; 84t AA/T Souter; 84bl AA/T Souter; 84br AA/P Kenward; 85 AA/P Kenward; 86 Courtesy of Turkish Culture & Tourist Office; 87 Courtesy of Turkish Culture & Tourist Office; 88 AA/C Sawyer; 89 Bon Appetit/Alamy; 90 AA/C Sawyer; 91 AA/T Souter; 94l Courtesy of Turkish Culture & Tourist Office; 94r AA/C Sawyer; 95l AA/C Sawyer; 95r AA/P Bennett; 96l AA/T Souter; 96tr Courtesy of Turkish Culture & Tourist Office; 96br AA/P Kenward; 97t Courtesy of Turkish Culture & Tourist Office; 97bl Courtesy of Turkish Culture & Tourist Office; 97br AA/C Sawyer; 98l AA/T Souter; 98c AA/C Sawyer; 98r AA/T Souter; 99t Courtesy of Turkish Culture & Tourist Office; 99bl AA/T Souter; 99br AA/T Souter; 100t Courtesy of Turkish Culture & Tourist Office; 100bl Courtesy of Turkish Culture & Tourist Office; 100br AA/C Sawyer; 101t Courtesy of Turkish Culture & Tourist Office; 101bl AA/C Sawyer; 101br AA/T Souter; 102 AA/C Sawyer; 103 AA/T Souter; 104t Courtesy of Turkish Culture & Tourist Office; 104b Photodisc; 105 AA/C Sawyer; 106 AA/C Sawyer; 107 Panoramic Images/Getty Images; 108t AA/C Sawyer; 108ct Photodisc; 108cc AA/T Souter; 108cb AA/T Souter; 108b AA/T Souter; 109 AA/C Sawyer; 110 AA/C Sawyer; 111 AA/C Sawyer; 112 AA/C Sawyer; 113 Courtesy of Turkish Culture & Tourist Office; 114 AA/P Kenward; 115 AA/P Kenward; 116t AA/P Kenward; 116b AA/P Kenward; 117 AA/P Kenward; 118 AA/P Kenward; 119 AA/P Kenward; 120 AA/P Kenward; 121t AA/P Kenward; 121b Courtesy of MRI Banker's Guide to Foreign Currency; 122 AA/P Kenward; 123 AA/P Kenward; 124t AA/P Kenward; 124bl Courtesy of Turkish Culture & Tourist Office; 124bc AA; 124br Courtesy of Turkish Culture & Tourist Office; 125t AA/P Kenward; 125bl AA/P Bennett; 125br Courtesy of Turkish Culture & Tourist Office.

Every effort has been made to trace the copyright holders, and we apologise in advance for any accidental errors. We would be happy to apply the corrections in the following edition of this publication.